EGGS IN COFFEE, SHEEP IN THE CORN

EGGS IN THE COFFEE, SHEEP IN THE CORN

My 17 Years as a Farmwife

Marjorie Myers Douglas

Minnesota Historical Society Press • St. Paul

Midwest Reflections
Memoirs and personal histories of the people of the Upper Midwest

Publication of this book was supported, in part, with funds
provided by the Elmer L. and Eleanor J. Andersen Publications
Endowment Fund of the Minnesota Historical Society

Minnesota Historical Society Press
St. Paul 55102

Manufactured in the United States of America
10 9 8 7 6 5 4 3 2 1

International Standard Book Number   0-87351-299-5 (paper)
                                      0-87351-300-2 (cloth)

The paper used in this publication meets the minimum
requirements of the American National Standard for
Information Sciences—Permanence for Printed Library
Materials, ANSI Z39.48-1984.

Library of Congress Cataloging-in-Publication Data
Douglas, Marjorie M.
     Eggs in the coffee, sheep in the corn : my 17 years as a farmwife
/ Marjorie Myers Douglas.
          p.   cm. — Midwest reflections
     ISBN 0-87351-300-2 (cloth : acid-free). — ISBN 0-87351-299-5
(paper : acid-free)
     1. Douglas, Marjorie M. 2. Farmers' spouses—Minnesota—
Appleton—Biography. 3. Farm life—Minnesota—Appleton.
4. Appleton (Minn.)—Biography. I. Title. II. Series.
S417.D7A3   1994
636.2'0092—dc20
[B]   94-17244
                                                            CIP

*Portions of chapters 23 and 27 appeared in a different version as "Easter Bottle Baby"
in Nancy Weber, ed.,* Cellar Doors and Hollyhocks: Writing by Older
Minnesotans *(St. Paul: COMPAS, 1986).*

*Frontispiece: Marjorie Myers at college graduation, 1933. Postcards reproduced on
pages 45 and 159 are used by courtesy of Robert Hayes. All other photographs are from
the collections of the author and her children.*

To my parents

Walter Raleigh Myers, a spinner of tales who never
wrote them down, and Olinia May Mattison Myers,
who always wanted him to.

Contents

Harvest 🖋

Preface

This book is a reminiscence of the years from 1943 to 1960, which I spent unexpectedly as a farmwife in western Minnesota. I had grown up in a professor's family in Minneapolis, abysmally ignorant of farming, and I had wrestled with our decision to leave the city for the stock farm near Appleton. I was not, however, entirely unwilling to go. While my husband Don felt obligated to help his parents during a time of crisis on their farm, he consulted me as to my feelings. Like so many women of my generation, I was already conditioned to follow his lead. Also, I can now freely confess, I was mildly curious about what I thought of as the active or "physical" life on a farm.

With a year-old daughter in diapers and no running water in the farmhouse, I soon found my curiosity satisfied. I quickly developed a real respect for people who can *do* things! Following their example, I learned to do things, too—bake bread, stake tomatoes, mother newborn animals, raise three lively children, and teach Sunday school. At the same time I watched in amazement as my husband demonstrated farming skills I had never seen and became a leader in the community.

This memoir does not presume to provide a commentary on social and economic conditions in rural Minnesota, nor on the business end of farming. Although I could surely offer opinions on these matters, I am not comfortable doing so—in some way I never stopped thinking of myself as the "kitchen help." I can illuminate only one point of view, that of an incurably optimistic city girl. I hope that my readers will feel they have sat at a farm kitchen table, laughed with the hired men and the children, and enjoyed yarning with the neighbors.

During those seventeen years, against the backdrop of hard work and constant worry about the weather, I heard stories of marvelous farm happenings. Other stories were told on me: how Marj, armed only with a dull ax, faced eighty-five hens and eventually won. And I began to understand how people in this midwestern farm neighborhood lived out the independence and steadfast moral sense so highly valued by Minnesotans.

I have dreamed of being a writer since I was in grade school, but as a child of the Depression, I prepared instead for a practical career. My adult life was always too busy for me to indulge in writing. But after my husband and I retired and an afternoon nap became part of his daily routine, I suddenly had a regular time to write. With the help of Don's memory and the entries I had made in my children's baby books, I developed quite a collection of stories.

As I became more serious about my work, I joined COMPAS and received invaluable help from the authors and teachers who worked there with Margaret Swanson. Carol Bly was my first editor. Her direct and honest approach made me realize I had hard work ahead of me, but she also encouraged me, and I began to think of composing the episodes I had written into a book. I also benefited from suggestions by Ian Leask and Jonis Agee. Margot Fortunato Galt then oversaw my project—with patience and insight—until it was ready for Ann Regan, managing editor at the Minnesota Historical Society Press. She and editor Ann Redpath paid meticulous attention to style and detail and stimulated me to evaluate this material in new ways.

I was also supported by a loving and frank neighborhood writing group. Zola Thompson, Mary Rogers, and Pat Denis read and commented on many of the chapters. Donna Opp gave me constant encouragement and, after my husband's death, Herbert Opp checked some practical farming details for me. Fred and Elizabeth Taylor read the manuscript, and their son-in-law, Steven Ronald, offered helpful editing tips. Tim Munkeby, Adree Bey, Marjorie and Don Erickson, Barbara and Bob Kerr, and Polly Bennett read early versions and made positive suggestions. Friends welcomed me into a writing class at Lynnhurst Community Center in Minneapolis and commented perceptively on chapters I read aloud there.

My children Anne, Bill, and Bruce enlarged my point of view as they helped me to remember the events of long ago. Bruce, Bill and his wife Kay, and my neighbors Julie de Witt and Kit Ketchum educated me in the mysteries of a word processor and printer and kept mine running.

All enriched my understandings, and to all I am deeply grateful.

Transplanted

Marjorie Douglas and Bumbly, 1943

Overleaf:
Donald Moats Douglas and Marjorie Myers Douglas, 1937

Horse Maids

M e? Feed a new baby colt? I'm the city gal who arrived on this bewildering piece of real estate
one week ago, remember?"

"You're doing great!" my husband grinned at me.
"You'll get a kick out of this—honest! The colt needs a
friend and will for a long time."

"But Don, I thought their mothers fed them."

"She died when he was born. Please? I got a bottle
ready while you were dressing Anne. Here's what you
do."

I had much in common with both colt and Anne, my
toddler daughter. Newly wrenched from our city home
near my parents, I felt almost as much an orphan as the
little work horse, and nearly as ignorant of every aspect of
farming as our daughter.

Bundled up against the cold, with her small hand eagerly grasping mine, we stepped into the cavernous hundred-foot barn. The big black horse in her stall startled
us with her trumpeting whinny. Teammate to the dead
mother, she moved nervously and stamped her hooves,
the hollow sound loud and echoing. The riding horse si-
dled expectantly to the front of the stall, but we ignored

him, not knowing whether this was a friendly overture inviting our caresses or a show of resentment at our intrusion. As my eyes grew used to the dimmer light, I spied the colt—a small spindly brown body on the yellowish straw near the manger. His big eyes fixed us in their gaze. We entered and timidly stroked his head, so wobbly on its slender neck. His legs worked convulsively, and suddenly he heaved himself up at the shoulders and gained his feet. I cautiously extended the Coca-Cola bottle with its huge nipple, but he let it slip away from his velvety muzzle. Remembering our instructions, I squirted a little of the diluted cow's milk onto his lips. Almost at once he was sucking greedily, noisily, happily. We laughed and scratched his head and rubbed his neck. He pushed against us, nuzzling. Anne crowed delightedly. He was ours. We were his.

After this, my new chores fell into place around the four bottles of milk a day this hungry baby enjoyed. Soon a ginger ale bottle replaced the Coke bottle and then a bucket. By spring Bumbly, as we called him, had grown to be a great friendly nuisance. We found him stumbling into my cherished row of peony bushes along the path to Papa and Mother Douglas's house and even climbing on Don's back when he worked on machinery in the yard. One day Bumbly clattered into the summer kitchen where Mother Douglas and I were washing clothes and plunged his muzzle into the foamy rinse water. Surely he must have thought he had reached Horse Heaven where milk comes in bottomless tubs, and he could live in the house with his humans.

He died at about five months of age, not of greed but of unpreventable navel disease that the veterinarian ex-

*Anne with the cat,
"Mama Mimi," and
her new litter of kittens
at the pump house*

plained was present from birth. Peonies still remind us of
him and his clumsy exuberance. At this point, I should
be able to describe a touching scene with all of us gathered to lay our pet away under a blanket of peonies. But
that would be pure fiction. Instead we called a truck with
the unmistakable label, "Dead Animal Service."
Anne asked for him constantly until I told her he and
his mother were together again. Then she discovered the
new litter of kittens. But whenever I thought of that helpless body huddled motionless in the corner of his stall,
with no sign of a struggle, a disproportionate sense of loss
swept over me. Suddenly I realized how lonely I was. To
my surprise, tears of angry frustration welled up over
being cut off from old friends and not finding new ones
in this place where I had not asked to be. I was adrift and
trying to adjust as my gentle parents had taught me, focusing on what I ought to do rather than my wants. I was
burying myself ever deeper in my new duties. The pleasure we had found in caring for Bumbly had softened my

overwhelming sadness at leaving our city "dreamhouse." Its sale had become final only a few months after we celebrated Anne's first birthday. In the five short months of Bumbly's life, I had learned to care and then begun to learn that I must be ready to let go, for the kaleidoscope of farm events turns rapidly. When the veterinarian found us a young black colt to take Bumbly's place, we declined. It would not have been the same.

I was definitely a product of the city, of Minneapolis. During my long courtship with Don, I had enjoyed tales of his farm upbringing but I was quite content to leave it at that. I could picture him as a tall, skinny lad trapping muskrats at the edge of the thin ice, or dozing confidently as his mount picked his way home through the swamp. I could see him, as Don described himself, being rescued by his brother from their "gentle" Jersey bull. Don told of how he had been knocked down by the bull, but had wriggled onto his back, partly protected by a stanchion. As the bull hulked over him, the massive head relentlessly squeezing the breath out of his rib cage, his brother grabbed a pitchfork and ran toward the bull, driving him off. I gave thanks that he had survived. Yet, Don's stories never gave me any idea of the practical side of farming, and I could not imagine ever wanting or needing to know more.

Then with sudden news of Papa Douglas's severe heart attack, all our plans changed and everything fell apart. Don left the Twin Cities immediately, traveling across the sandy, flat landscape of western Minnesota to the Douglases' big stock ranch near Appleton to assess the situation and help his mother make immediate plans. He returned convinced that without our help—physical and financial—his parents would almost certainly lose the ranch. Though they were once wealthy, Papa's heavy hospital expenses—as well as his inability to work—put them in a perilous situation. Papa had seen the business of farming begin to pick up again after the stock market crash and the dust bowl of the thirties. He had believed he could make a big success of this place but needed cash to keep going. Reluctantly, we made our decision to join forces with Papa and Mother Douglas—William Stephen A. (known as W.S.A.) and Vivian—for perhaps a year or two. When the local draft board, more concerned in 1943 for food for a nation enmeshed in World War II than for bullets, approved the move, I knew this impossible nightmare was reality. As soon as Don could train in a new man to take his place at the armaments plant, he hurried back to the farm. Still dazed, I was left to sell the house. During those forlorn months from August 1943 to February 1944, when I was alone with Anne, the sunshine that flooded our modern kitchen more than once revealed tears of self-pity on my cheeks. As I emptied kitchen cupboards, Anne would ride her second-hand Taylor Tot past me, snatch up a package of Jell-O or a can of soup, and laughingly scuttle off. Then around she came past the half-bath and basement recreation room door to elude me again.

I pondered over everything I learned in Don's phone calls, hasty visits, and letters, but still I could not think myself into the unknown life of a farmwife. In my ignorance I could not get beyond the picture of simply caring for my husband and child in new surroundings. Surely I wouldn't be carrying slop to hogs, would I? Reared in the provincialism of the academic community, I could not imagine life that did not center on ideas. Would the small town of Appleton, three and a half miles east of the farm, offer any kind of social and intellectual stimulation? A miasma of doubts and nameless fears confronted me. My usually dependable stomach turned unreliable, and my sleep was broken as on that long ago night when the train carried me away from everything familiar to New York City and my first job out of college. For that work I had been prepared, but what could I contribute on a farm? And what would it mean for Don's career and for our child?

Finally, we sold our suburban town house and, after five months apart, Don moved us to the farm. We were happy indeed to be living together again, but before I was used to our new surroundings, the compelling routine of hearty meals began to make rude inroads on my time with our daughter. Whenever we had extra help on the farm, Mother Douglas and I prepared the meal in my big kitchen, and we all ate together.

Suddenly I had to learn to cook and clean without running water. How could I complain about the plumbing when Mother Douglas and Papa—who by this time was home from the hospital and improving slowly—happily insisted on moving to one of the houses for hired help? There she presided as graciously as she had in larger houses when their fortunes were far different. She and Don had even stolen time to paint and paper the comfortable six-room home for us before I joined Don there.

To do our laundry, Mother Douglas and I carried water from the pump, which stood across the dooryard and the driveway, between the stock tank and the garden.

Anne helps to carry water from the pump

We heated it in a copper boiler on an old wood-burning cookstove in the summer kitchen. I remembered jokes about frozen one-piece union suits, but now I was not amused as I hung them steaming on the line and later struggled to carry them back to the house, stiff and only half dry, as dark closed in. Sometimes Don managed to finish chores early. Then, after a bedtime romp and a song with Anne, he helped me finish my work, and we laughed without any need for jokes, glad just to be together.

But I found I had also to adjust to the demands the

heavy work and Papa's directions made on my husband's time and energy. One day, early that first winter, I went with Don to watch his outside chores. While it was a foreign world to me, I hoped vaguely that I could assist. A wide flat belt from the noisy tractor drove the hammer-mill, and Don kept warning me of its danger. He told of farmers whose clothes got caught in the belt and were stripped off. Sometimes bones were broken—or worse. He shoveled in screenings and balancer to make the correct mix for stock feed, and soon a great cloud of dust had me coughing. I was amazed at all the things he knew how to do so skillfully.

Every day or two, he loaded up a big wagon with sixty-five-pound bales of hay for the steers in the pasture that now was covered with snow. I could not begin to lift one and only slowed him up when I tried to help. I was determined to see the soon-to-be-farrowing sows he tended so carefully, but my alien presence in the hog house disturbed the sows. I could tell that Don was uneasy, both for me and for his precious animals. Now I understood his getting up at night to check on the heavy mothers that sometimes smothered the piglets by rolling on them, or unpredictably turned nervous and ate their progeny or charged their keepers. I started to lie awake rigid with vivid imaginings until he returned to our bed, chilled but cheerful and reassuringly full of life.

One morning, after such a night, I stepped out onto the front porch into blinding bright sunshine. My back was to the busy dooryard and the main Milwaukee tracks that paralleled Highway 7. Tracks and highway followed roughly the old Yellowstone Trail, bisecting the ranch. To reach the cropland the men had to drive the machinery half a block north up our driveway, across the railroad tracks, then follow the highway a short distance to enter the fields on one of two narrow trails. Everything to the south was peaceful today as I looked over the parklike expanse, glistening with a late snowfall. It stretched from the vigorous old cottonwood branching over the house to a distant fence that divided lawn from river pasture. The scene called out an insistent invitation.

As soon as breakfast was over, Anne and I abandoned the kitchen chores and ventured out—she in her homemade red snowsuit, I in ski pants and plaid mackinaw. Our feet in their galoshes made a big trail and a little trail on the clean snow. When we turned to look back, the tracks had mysteriously filled with blue and purple shadows. Like two light-hearted children, we kicked up great clouds of powdery snow that shimmered in the sunlight. Anne stumbled and fell and was unsure whether to laugh or cry as the sparkling stuff melted on her rosy cheeks and slid under the scarf around her neck. I fell down beside her, and we imprinted our private park with "angels," tall and wobbly and short and fat. Soon Anne grew tired. Reluctantly we turned home. That day, I could not have guessed how infrequently we would use that yard or that porch once the snow was gone.

It was the fall of 1944 before I remember really catching my breath to take stock of my situation. I was losing my reliance on orderly planning and was learning to take things as they came. I had even undertaken to can five gunnysacks of delicious windfall apples that neighbors had offered us from their bumper crop of Wealthies.

While Anne napped, I sat on a high stool at the kitchen sink to begin coring and sectioning apples to cook up, put through a small hand-cranked sieve, and can. For a moment my courage failed me at the vastness of the job. I could feel my body slump as I looked out the north window at the young cottonwood tree draped with Heavenly Blue morning glories escaping from the fence. Papa called it "Marj's bloomin' cottonwood tree," but the teasing edge to his voice told me he had no idea what its beauty meant to me.

I closed my eyes. The sound of the fluttering leaves became the waves lapping on the shore of my mother and dad's island cottage. I was a little girl again, dangling my feet in the cool waters of Lake Minnetonka. My father, a professor of German at the University of Minnesota, took joy in my every achievement, especially my love of books. I came by that naturally. He had wooed my mother from her work at Northwestern University Library. I was the middle child between capable, dependable Bob and mischievous Everett. In summers Dad, who truly loved to teach, taught the family, and even friends, how to swim, play tennis, and boat. We met other canoes for songfests by moonlight or fished near the reeds on the point. I grew lithe and brown.

My mind jumped to the year I met Don, when I was a mere junior in high school, and he a sophomore at the University of Minnesota. I remembered acutely his laughing, animated presence behind me in the bass section of the choir where I sang a timid soprano. He was tall and handsome, and his large blue eyes gave me a feeling of utter trust. On our first date, he decided that he would marry me (though I didn't hear about that until much later).

He waited for me for nine long years during the Great

Marjorie's parents, Walter and Olinia Myers, early 1930s

Marjorie at Lake Minnetonka, near her parents' cottage

Depression while I finished college and proved myself—
an "insurance policy" my parents insisted upon. Although marriage and child rearing was the expected role
for women at that time, they wanted me to be independent if anything should happen to whomever I married. I
had gone to New York City as a medical social worker at
Columbia Presbyterian Medical Center. Another new social worker, Miriam Flexner, and I lived in a third-floor
walk-up apartment across from Charles Schwab's estate
on Riverside Drive. There, we explored this fabulous
city's museums, theaters, and ethnic restaurants together. I had felt Don and I should not be officially engaged
when we were to be separated for such a long time, but
every letter or gift of flowers I received from him was
signed "Always, Don." And so it proved to be. Two years
later I left for a job in St. Paul with the new novel *Gone
with the Wind* under my arm, a going-away gift from
friends who correctly guessed that I would be married
the next spring to my first love.

On June 19, 1937, one hundred guests crowded into
my parents' home to hear our marriage vows. Just as the
minister was asking if anyone knew any reason why we
should not be joined in holy matrimony, the phone jan-
gled stridently. It rang only once because Everett, who
was standing near, snatched it off the hook. He held the
receiver unanswered while a surprised friend, wanting
only to apologize for being unable to attend, listened as
the ceremony concluded in peace.

At that time, I was busy with the responsibilities of setting up a social work department at Gillette State Hospital for Crippled Children, and I continued my work there
until Anne was on the way in 1942. Hard times had

brought great demand for social workers everywhere, so jobs were plentiful.

How different Don's work experience had been. While I was in New York City, he had set up and lost a small printing business when his partner absconded with the profits. He worked several temporary jobs to pay off a company debt of several thousand dollars, and times in between were lean. Then he joined the Federal Land Bank as a field man but quit when he found his work consisted mostly of foreclosing government loans on small farmers. His college work had been in engineering and business, but engineers were being laid off everywhere. Finally he found congenial work with the new Soil Conservation Service. There his jovial, sincere approach softened suspicious farmers, and he drew on his own farm background to help develop and implement this much-needed program. The contour farming technique soon began to hold topsoil in the hills around Faribault, and Don enjoyed making new converts as the program spread. By 1941 he was contributing to the war effort at the Twin Cities Ordnance Plant by supervising two shifts of inspectors. He had no apparent desire to return to making a living on the land. In fact, before our marriage, I used to tease Don about writing up a marriage contract to stipulate we would *never* live on a farm.

What if I had really done that? Would it have changed anything? Before Papa's heart attack, our life together had seemed the living out of our dreams—especially after waiting nine long years. At home in the city, the cultural centers were close by, and we were near our old friends and my parents, who delighted in their first grandchild. Our large new house, across the road from the tidy fields

Don and Marjorie's "dream house" on New Brighton Road, 1942

of the university's agriculture campus, occupied a one-acre lot—plenty of space for Don's garden and my flowers. Our daughter Anne arrived, completing all our dreams. This move to the farm was a disruption of everything we had worked and prepared for. Or could I be wrong about this? Could it be that I had let Don make too many sacrifices? Had I asked too much adjustment from the farming life he had grown up with? His only brother, Glenn, had married Lillian Bagstad from Benson and settled on a farm near there; now he was independent and raising a family. Don was the only one of his generation to break away from farm life—a decision that many more young people were making. Was there a part of him that clung to farming as a way to support his family?

I knew my parents regarded the move to the Douglas ranch as a calamity, but, respecting our right to choose, they said nothing. They loved Don like a son and valued his wholehearted, honest, loving ways, but they knew they had not raised their only daughter to be a farmer's wife. I had slipped easily from their protective love to his, but now I was struggling to be firm in supporting his loyalty to his parents.

The meager infusion of capital that we brought to the enterprise represented only our small savings, equity in our home, and some life insurance. Yet it gave Papa his only recourse. Farm managers were virtually unknown in that area and, even if he could have found one, he could never have afforded the salary. Manpower of any sort was in short supply with so many in the army. Each day now I understood better why a 1,200-acre stock ranch could not be left to casual help. The Douglas farm had one hundred head of cattle on feed, hogs nearly ready for market, three hundred acres of hay waiting in the meadow, grain soon to turn, and then corn to ripen. It was good that Don, at six feet six inches, had been a swimmer and a football player, for now his considerable energies were consumed in dawn-to-dark physical labor. But how long would this have to continue? And why us? At that time, Don did not tell me that he hoped a successful farming experience would mean a solid financial start for us, wherever we decided to settle. I did know quite clearly that he wanted a second chance for his parents.

I came to with a start when the knife dropped from my hands at the sink, bringing me back to reality. Hurriedly, I tackled the mountain of apples, but I could not escape my thoughts. Dreams long cherished do not give way easily. In spite of myself, the Heavenly Blue morning glories teased my gaze back to the window. It occurred to me that it must be just as hard for Papa to have his dreams interrupted so abruptly. Robust, vigorous, always in charge, he must have felt overwhelmed by his sudden helplessness. And yet, somehow, it was not quite like that. I tried to identify what puzzled me. His figure seemed a little shrunken perhaps, since his illness, although the swell of his midriff still emphasized his strong frame. His face was thinner—that was it. But helpless he was not! He tentatively acquiesced in the doctor's instructions under his wife's watchful care. One always had the feeling, however, that Papa intended to order his affairs exactly as he wished. His fine eyes bulged a little under brows bristling with long white hairs. His well-defined features were a bit heavier than Don's, and his posture even at the table commanded attention. His voice—whether teasing, giving orders, or telling his interminable stories—overcame any competition. Don once commented that Papa had developed this story-telling habit to his advantage when he was buying and selling farm real estate. It kept the buyer off guard, while Papa's busy mind calculated and rephrased his offer until it was accepted.

My uneasiness persisted. Papa was a bit overbearing, but it was more than that. If he had dealt so cleverly with his business customers, how could I be sure that he was being entirely open and straightforward with us? Don was caught up in trying to fill in all the gaps—stockman, crop consultant, machinery expert, negotiator, and laborer—while I found myself feeling guilty when my hands were idle for a few minutes. Anne's wake-up cry came from upstairs. I stepped away from the sink, apples barely started, and called to her while I began to set out the playpen. I knew she would protest the confinement, but it would be necessary as I handled the steaming, bubbling applesauce. The blue of the morning glories again caught my eye as I hurried about. What early memories would Anne have of her physical home? Not lapping waves and elm trees on high bluffs like my summers, not friendly city streets and parks in a close neighborhood like the school years of my childhood. Perhaps these flat sandy plains, where all the roads proceeded in straight lines and no hills or valleys broke the monotony, would "look like home" to her someday. I determined they would at least be dotted with bright splashes of Heavenly Blue, if indeed we remained here another year. And I felt sure I had an ally in town-reared Mother Douglas. Always sensitive and gracious, she sometimes seemed intensely aware of me and my reactions as if appraising what this decision meant to me, but neither of us put anything into words. Did she suspect that I sometimes felt as much an orphan as the colt Anne and I had mothered?

A Shift in the Wind

One unaccountably hazy dawn that spring, I woke to find Don already up and at the bedroom window alarmed by the strong wind. It came purposefully from the north across the newly planted fields, its exploring fingers stirring the pulverized soil and lightly lifting it to ride the air currents.

This was the day a social worker from the county seat at Benson had arranged to interview me about one of the Douglases' former employees, who now lived in California. I was eager to visit with a fellow social worker, for already my years in that profession seemed as if they were in the distant past.

"I wonder if Nancy Jacobsen will come in such a bad wind?" I worried aloud.

"I s'pose. Prob'ly."

Had Don really heard me? His concern for the crops made him see the wind as an evil threat. He gulped his breakfast and, without even stopping to shave, raced on his tractor to the field. With his cultivator he scraped up ridges of dirt every few rows, trying to protect the small seedlings that had begun to green the fields. The velocity of the wind kept increasing, and soon Papa and the hired man began working the nearby acres also. In spite of their efforts, by noon the wind had stolen a rich dark treasure of topsoil.

During the dust storms of the mid-thirties, relentless winds had literally blown the crops out of the ground, dried out the pastures, and in places piled up the soil from the fields over the tops of the fences. Animals had to be sold, for there was no feed. Even the chickens, turned loose to forage for themselves, barely subsisted on what they could find. Our neighbors, the Cairnses, had told us about retreating to their basement, stuffing newspapers into the cracks around windows and doors to keep out the grit. The bawling of the few remaining starving steers, which they'd soon have to slaughter for meat, had driven the Cairnses almost to distraction. During this difficult era, the government initiated many programs as part of the Works Progress Administration. Needy farmers contributed skills to building a park by the Pomme de Terre dam, as well as other improvements in the community. Of course, the farmers were joined by workmen and small business owners, for when the farmers had no money, the economy of this farm town ground to a halt.

I hated the wind, but never before had I experienced its vicious destructiveness. At this time of year the fields were so open and vulnerable. I wanted to cower inside the house and not expose my face and arms to its gritty menace. When I ventured out, I snatched up a jacket to protect myself and tied a scarf over my hair. At the same time, I wished I could protect in my hands the tender shoots of corn to give them a chance to live.

By the middle of the afternoon, when the social

worker braved the savage gusts in her stylish suit and heels and reached the farmhouse door, I, like the men in the field, felt anxious and on edge. How much would have to be replanted? Would it be too late in the season to get a good crop?

With Anne napping and an applesauce cake in the oven, I ushered Miss Jacobsen into the quiet comfort of the living room. I found I could contribute very little to the information she had already gathered, so our talk turned to each other. She had moved to Minneapolis from a small town on the Iron Range in northern Minnesota to get her training. She felt she had tasted all the excitement Benson could offer. While she was ready for a livelier scene, she was not sure that she would get a good job because of her limited training and experience. She questioned me about New York City and my life there. How dangerous was it to make home visits in Harlem? Were the plays at Times Square very expensive? Who had been my date when I danced on the roof garden of the Biltmore Hotel? How much had my trip to Bermuda cost?

It surprised me that Miss Jacobsen asked no questions about the ethnic groups in the burgeoning city, or what resources were available for them. She also showed no interest in my lament about the schools, drowning under the flood of poor children. Realizing how behind I was on professional news—as I ached for time to read—I eagerly questioned her, but she deftly changed the subject.

At nearly four o'clock, Anne woke all pink and warm with tight damp curls clinging to her neck. I dressed her, and she and Miss Jacobsen entertained each other while I prepared the coffee, cut the warm cake, and set the table. Papa, Don, and the hired man would join the three of us. The roar of the tractors blew ahead of them to announce their arrival. Hurriedly, they entered the cozy shelter of the kitchen, a blast of dirt-laden air rushing past them. Gloves, caps, and jackets stiff with grime were shed and dropped just inside the door. Their hands without their gloves looked almost white, but not their faces! Usually I felt a thrill of pride when I introduced my husband, but today the men looked unreal as if they had donned blackface for a play. Don was the worst of the lot. His whiskers held the soil on his cheeks and chin, making him look like a coal miner.

While our guest didn't actually cringe, Miss Jacobsen was careful to keep her distance. It was a quiet, not very sociable gathering. The men made a few labored attempts at conversation, but they were ill at ease and distracted. By now, they knew that they would lose much of the planting in spite of their efforts. So they quickly finished their food and made their getaway to face the cutting wind again. I was acutely aware of our guest's discomfort, but I was still more surprised at this social worker's lack of tact.

When the door closed behind the men, who left little piles of dirt on the floor where their coats had been, Nancy Jacobsen's first remark was, "Do you mean to say you left a good career in social work for—for—*this?*"

Quick anger flashed. This was *my* husband, *my* darling child, *my* father-in-law she was disparaging. What gave her the right? She was a guest in my house, at my table, and she had the nerve to denigrate my whole way of life?

I hoped my outrage did not show, though I felt my cheeks burn. My heart pounded with an effort to choke back furious, hurtful words that I knew would be useless. I saw before me an unmarried, childless woman with her youth fading. Listening to her speak that afternoon, I was sure she was not gaining much satisfaction from her chosen work. Why had she made me so angry? Perhaps I secretly coveted her opportunities in my profession, yet I felt indignant that she was treating my current work so lightly. From her tactless question I sensed her unhappiness, and I pitied her hunger for something more satisfying. I remember mumbling some cliché about each person's right to choose, but my voice sounded stilted and tight in my throat. When she left, I think we both felt relieved.

Suppose we did have to endure a dismal job on a dirty day like this once in a while, I argued in my mind as she drove away. We were together, we were slowly getting ahead, and we were happy. Some pleasant memories of my social work had been revived by our conversation. But the career, I realized, had never been uppermost for me. Everything I had learned as a social worker—about bringing out the best in people—I could use in the life Don and I were building together. Not just in our family, but in the community, too. In this moment of insight I saw myself as the happy, loved, and contributing farmwife. But I still couldn't understand why I was so shaken by the disdain of this small-town woman.

Farming——The Sinister Side

To farm is to join with the sun and rain to bring seeds to glorious fruition, right? Well, maybe not so glorious. I never put it to Papa Douglas quite that way. Had I wanted to wax romantic, however, I'm sure he would have squinted his prominent blue eyes at me and enjoyed teasing me with tales of farming's many problems. He'd have made light of the pests and hailed-out crops, and the hard work that never lets up. He'd have thrown in the account of a drought or two and joked, "That's just the good Lord keeping you on your toes!" I'm sure he'd also have plunged into a story about theft—another dark side of farming. A farmer is exposed to more hazards than sun and rain, I learned. With stock, crops, and machinery spread out over many acres, the thief can often work undetected.

As a young man in Iowa, Papa built up a large prosperous farm. With his impressive six-foot stature, he became known in the community as one who liked to "think big." He kept many schemes going, including a small factory for producing cornhangers—his invention for drying the best corn for seed. Papa had helped several hired men start farming on their own by lending them money, guar-

anteeing their loans at the bank, or by sharing his machinery. When land values were rapidly increasing, he
sold the farm at a good profit and moved his family to
Storm Lake, where he did well with a farm real-estate
business. Soon he owned land throughout the Midwest.
He then joined other speculators in moving to Minnesota, where land was cheaper. Sometimes using options,
he spread his capital to its limit and was able to enter
comfortable semiretirement at Lake Minnewashta near
the Twin Cities.

But as farm credit tightened before the crash of 1929,
Papa was unable to keep control of his investments and
barely salvaged one of his larger farms—four hundred
acres of good, heavy land near Benson. Don and his
brother, Glenn, were in high school when they moved to
the Benson farm; Papa and Mother Douglas were still living on this farm when I met Don. The family cared for

The Douglas farm house at Benson, Minnesota

eighty Jersey cows, without the use of milking machines, and Papa had a milk delivery route in town. The boys shared the drudgery of hand milking for hours before and after school. For years afterwards they told jokes about that dairy route—such as the one about hearty Mrs. Peterson who wanted "fresh morning's milk" with "lots of cream on top." To provide her that cream, the milk had to be day-old, so that the rich yellow Jersey cream could rise and fill the bottle all the way to the shoulder. Repeated explanations had no effect on the lady, so they devised a plan to keep her happy.

"Hey, come back with that milk," they would sing out as the boy who was delivering off the truck approached her gate. "Mrs. Peterson gets this fresh milk."

The identical bottles were promptly exchanged and, satisfied that her order was special, she proudly quoted their slogan, "You can whip our cream, but you can't beat our milk!"

Years later, after both sons were married and Don had finished college, Papa and Vivian sold their equity in that farm, which carried an unduly heavy tax burden because it was included in the town school district. In addition, Papa's extensive ditching work created a ditch tax. In the early 1940s they moved to the much larger, but less en-cumbered, stock ranch at Appleton. There the excellent pasture sloped a mile to the Pomme de Terre River, but some of its cropland was lighter and sandy. They had been there three years when Don and little Anne and I hastily joined them after Papa's heart attack. He was still strong and quick, although years of eating his wife's fa-mous cooking had thickened his waist and slowed his step.

In his first year there, Papa offered two young hired men a chance to make extra money by raising chickens in their spare time. He paid for three hundred pullets, and the men, all too eagerly, agreed to care for them and give Papa half the profit. Unfortunately the chickens began to disappear with great regularity, and the men's excuses were transparent.

"That time I just bet on a couple of losers," Papa philosophized. "Nothing ventured, nothing gained."

He must have recognized that his holding was the biggest in the area, although it was definitely less productive than the Benson land. In this setting, his well-equipped farm was a target for theft.

His lenience may have been a grave mistake, for, by the time we became partners, theft and "borrowing" had developed into a real problem. We even wondered if the Douglases had been branded easy marks.

I think Don saw theft as just another problem requiring action, but for me it was unsettling, isolated as I was and unfamiliar with every aspect of the environment. Certainly dishonesty did not fit with my vague ideas of rural folks as simple, hard working, and God fearing.

The first thing we lost was gasoline. Gasoline, like money, is a universal commodity. Everyone needs it, it is everywhere available, and one gallon is indistinguishable from another. If it is stolen, there is no easy way to identify it or to know where it came from. Each farm has a big tank. Ours held six hundred gallons of field gasoline on which the road tax was forgiven. Its use was restricted to farm machinery. In the spring the bulk oil man always came out with his immense fuel truck and filled our tank.

Several times that spring Don remarked that the level

in the tank had gone down faster than he could explain. This happened when we were all at church or on the rare evenings we were away. He fastened his suspicions on a young farmer who rented a neighboring 160-acre farm of light sandy soil that barely supported his family. We knew this man to be wily because, during the previous winter, he had pried up a fence where our fat sows were gleaning our cornfield. He had used his boar to lure them into his hog lot, then boldly claimed three as his own. It is difficult to face a thief with nothing but your word against his. Papa, for all his bluster, would have nothing to do with it. Don felt just as strongly that now was the time to take a stand. He had always measured his dealings with others by the creed of fairness, but fairness had to work both ways.

Don confronted the young neighbor but was unsuccessful in retrieving the stolen sows until he called in the sheriff. Luckily, the sheriff had seen the trick used before and recognized the tell-tale signs by the disturbance of the fence and the tracks in the soft ground. The sows were returned home, but a nagging distrust lingered. What kind of neighborhood had I come into, I wondered. If we stayed here, who would be my children's companions? Would I ever find friends?

Now with cultivating in full swing, the gasoline continued to disappear at a rapid rate. Without the stolen fuel, our young neighbor's car and tractors would have been useless. Like Papa, we hesitated to confront anyone until we had solid evidence. Yet we could not let the situation go on indefinitely. Convinced that his surmise was correct, Don made discreet inquiries at the gas stations in town and of the bulk dealer. The young neighbor had made no gasoline purchases at all, though he was farming a quarter section and his old green Chevy was often seen on the road to Correll.

Meeting him by chance in town one day, Don came right to the point. "I've been losing a helluva lot of gas lately. It's going to stop."

It did stop. For us, that is. For our lanky neighbor friend Ed, however, stealing began the next day on his farm just east of us. Knowing Don's experience, Ed had a plan ready and was cocky and sure of success. "I'm moving a cot to a first-floor room overlooking the driveway and the gas tank," he told us. "I'll just open the window and sleep there. I'll stash my loaded rifle beside me, and make short work of him. You'll see."

"Good luck!" Don offered heartily. This man was an excellent and enthusiastic farmer. By the time he went to bed at night, he was thoroughly tired. He slept very soundly. And when he slept, he snored. Not a ladylike, rasping breath, but a heavy, window-rattling, buzz-saw snore. A thief could operate with impunity as long as the racket continued. Any cessation would be a warning. Shamefaced, our neighbor later admitted that when morning came the rifle was untouched, but not the gasoline. The level had gone down by what he judged to be ten gallons, a convenient amount to be carried away in two five-gallon cans. This was repeated the next night and the next. He had to concede temporary defeat.

Immediately, Ed set about devising another plan that he divulged to Don and Papa Douglas. This involved a clever but cruel contraption. His fuel tanks stood about six feet off the ground. The hose looped up on a spring a few feet above the tanks, just over the spot where a person would have to stand to release the gas. From this loop he suspended a short rope with a bottle of concentrated, itchy, smelly fly spray.

Night came with no moon. In the faint starlight, the determined man could barely discern the dark shape of the fly spray bottle against the lighter sky. Feeling that his reputation as a man of action was on the line, Ed forced himself to stay awake until he heard the sound he had been waiting for—the rush of gasoline into a can. Taking precise aim, he shattered the bottle with one rifle bullet. Incredibly, there was no other sound—no scream, no running feet, no upset gas cans. Obviously he had hit his mark. How could the plan have failed? He had to contain his impatience until morning when the first light told the story. In the driveway, clearly outlined by the whitish fly spray, was the shape of a stooping man. Success! The ruse would have been entirely worthy of Papa, who relished every detail and chuckled as he insisted on hearing it over and over. In this neighbor he recognized a fellow inventor.

Somewhat the worse for lack of sleep, but fiendishly gleeful, Ed hurried to town that morning and again in the afternoon. He hoped to hear about, or even encounter, someone suffering from severe burning and itching of the back and shoulders. Though disappointed, he couldn't help but feel a reluctant admiration. The thief had heard a rifle shot at close range, then the crash of breaking glass over his head, and endured a fiery baptism without an outcry to give him away. We could hardly hope that so sophisticated a thief was cured, but we did not hear of systematic theft of gasoline in our neighborhood again.

Don, right, with his father and mother, 1941

Hybrid Me

By the end of the first year we had become full partners with Don's folks. Although we gave farming our
utmost effort and put every nickel back into the business, somehow I still managed to think of it as temporary.
For what seemed like a long time after moving to Appleton, I felt I was a transplanted city girl, a hybrid too busy
learning to farm to get to know the community.

Even so, it soon became my turn to entertain the
Women's Society of the First Methodist Church. I had
learned to make egg coffee, mixing the ground beans
with a raw egg. I stirred this mixture into boiling water
and allowed it to boil up, then simmer a few minutes. Finally a dash of cold water made the grounds sink. But as I
put the pot on the stove, one of the ladies left the meeting and bustled into the kitchen. She tied a dark plaid
apron around her stout middle and exclaimed, "Oh no,
not *your* water!"

Before my startled, untutored eyes she produced a
church coffeepot full of town water. Our water was a bit
cloudy from the blue clay layer where the deep well shaft
ended. But how did they know? Then I realized that
many of these ladies had lived in the community since

childhood and had known our home for years as the "old Lang farm." At that moment an unfamiliar and uncomfortable feeling assailed me—I was still a newcomer and a novice in my own home.

A few days after that, as Don dashed through the kitchen on the way to pick up a badly needed repair in town, I innocently asked him to buy some rickrack at the dry-goods store for a dress I was finishing for Anne. I then sat down to phone a list of women for the next church circle meeting. After five or six calls, the operator's voice that had been asking, "Number, please?" in the accustomed impersonal way, startled me by suddenly coming to life.

"Listen, Marj," she began matter of factly, "your husband has been trying to reach you for ten minutes, and from the sound of him, I'd get off the line if I were you and give him a chance!"

She plugged him in, and I repeated the details of the errand I had thoughtlessly put ahead of the farm work. The operator, it turned out, was the friendly, talkative woman who sat in front of us at church the Sunday before.

I continued to enjoy the rich, rewarding relationship that was developing as Mother Douglas taught me to tend the garden, can produce, and make lavish meals for the farm crews in my big kitchen.

She used to say, "A farm runs on food. Gasoline for the tractors, and food—lots of it—for the people. They work hard and deserve the best."

I remember her quiet insistence on a large casserole of macaroni and cheese besides the tremendous amounts of pork roast and potatoes with glazed carrots, fresh peas, sliced tomatoes, and homemade bread and pie as noon dinner for the threshers.

Blushing even now, I recall my horrified protest: "You already have plenty of carbohydrates, Mother." (After all, I had studied dietary requirements at school!) "Well," she had smiled, "It's just a filler."

As I watched the macaroni disappear, along with all her delicious cooking, I began to value her wisdom and the renown she already enjoyed in Appleton for her bountiful table. Don told of a year when times were so hard at their Benson home that she had nothing to offer threshers every noon but mutton. I knew that mutton has a strong flavor and the tendency for its fat to congeal unappetitizingly on plate, tongue, and palate. Her sleight of hand with hot platters and seasonings was such that none guessed they were not eating beef until she told them at the end of the week. One of that crew who had always said he couldn't eat mutton hastily left the table and stepped outside.

"On the farm you'll never get rich, but you'll always eat well," was Papa's comment.

Papa was more difficult for me. To myself, I called him "Mr. Big." His recovery now allowed him to participate in all but the heaviest work. For that he still depended on Don. But though he relied on his son, I began to notice with some alarm that Mr. Big kept firm control of planning. After a full year had passed, he continued to make plans that would be unworkable without Don's help. Was this deliberate? Was he counting on our staying indefinitely? Don kept his own counsel. His relationship with his father had never been easy. I chose not to comment, but I became increasingly concerned.

I was also annoyed that Papa felt free to relate to Anne in his own way rather than deferring to our methods of training her. He relished his snatches of time with her at meals or when, to her joy, he took her to town on errands. He teased her and indulged her, and insisted, "Children are for parents to raise and grandparents to spoil." Instead of discouraging her misdeeds, he let her see his amusement when she was saucy or willful. I managed to hold my tongue except to remonstrate about ice cream cones just before dinner. Mother Douglas must have sensed my displeasure, for she shared her remembered fury when he had taken Don as a toddler to town, got into a business deal, and completely forgotten the boy. Papa came home without him!

Anne's vocabulary mushroomed amazingly, and I worried that she would not get all the mental nourishment she deserved without the concerts, children's plays, and social groups we had left behind. Consequently I probably overwhelmed her with what I could provide—books and companionship. When I talked with Abigail, a friend from church, about gates in doorways and stepping over Anne and her kettles and toys, she responded plainly: "How come you fence your kid in? I fence mine out!"

I fenced Anne in because I enjoyed her company and our conversations. Her imagination and curiosity blossomed as she would set an ailing doll tenderly next to the cake I was mixing and address me as "Dokytor." Two minutes later, I became Winnie-the-Pooh, or a driver of a "kwaktor" in the field, or even a "naughty cow." Naturally, she also grew in independence. Putting her slender foot into an overshoe from the pile beside the outside door, she would single-mindedly do battle with rusty buckles or a sand-encrusted zipper, and fend off my proffered help with cries of "No, no, no! I do it all by self."

Although I found pleasure in the faithfully tended garden, and Anne and I had once or twice enjoyed wading in the pretty little river while Don mended fence, nothing in the windy flat country approached the loveliness of the lake island I had lived on near the Twin Cities. In fact, it was not until the spring of 1945 that a sense of delight and belonging began to stir in me. That day the sun was shining, and I defected for a moment from the bewildering array of duties to wander into the small grassy, fenced-in yard. In the middle, a huge buckeye tree gleamed with great clusters of white blossoms. Its spreading seven-fingered leaves shadowed black-green against the hot blue sky.

As I gazed, three, then four, small iridescent creatures (we later identified them as mothhummingbirds) appeared. In a proprietary way, they thrust their long bills greedily into one floret after another. I watched entranced. On fanning wings, they harvested methodically, starting with the top of the towering tree. As they exhausted one cluster of flowers, they darted backward like true hummingbirds and hung motionless in midair while selecting another. I had hardly time to marvel at the flashing tiny bodies before they buried themselves in the next bloom. The following day they were gone and did not reappear until the false dragonshead opened its showy purple array in the fall. I have only to close my eyes today to enjoy again that dazzling sunlit scene and the thrill of awakening to this beauty in our own dooryard.

Were there other busy housewives finding joy and beauty in what I had imagined to be drab, isolated farm homes, I wondered. Had these women known each other at school? Did they ever get together as families for fun? Our neighbor Ed had two lively little girls about Anne's age, whom we had met briefly when grocery shopping one day, but we had not seen them since. With Don's parents older and not inclined to become involved in the church or social life of this town, we were outside this human network except for business and the Methodist church where we had become members.

Kitchen Help

From cornstalks to pressure cooker to Mason jars—in only three hours. I loaded up a tray with this precious cargo and carried it down the worn cellar steps with no bannister to guide me. I placed my feet with care as I trudged again and again to the murky basement. Tiny tender kernels caught the light through the greenish glass.

Twenty beautiful golden quarts had crowded the kitchen table as they cooled overnight. Now I arranged them on the shelf, leaving space ready for the next lot. One hundred quarts of string beans and one hundred of tomatoes, fifty each of rhubarb sauce and pickles, already crowded the shelf above.

Yesterday Don had offered to pick before he went to the field. Early morning found us facing overflowing bushel baskets of fresh sweet corn. Tearing away the coarse green shucks was noisy work, but Mother Douglas and I had no trouble chatting above the racket. Anne amused herself stacking and restacking the pale yellow ears after we rolled them in our hands and picked out the shiny clinging silks.

"Let's double-cut this batch," Mother Douglas suggested.

She taught me to stand each ear on end in a shallow pan and slice lengthwise repeatedly, bisecting the little kernels but leaving the hulls and then gently scraping the milky residue into the pan. The scene grew chaotic as we became daubed to the elbows with the sticky milk. The phone rang repeatedly with farm business, and the memos we wrote for the men were barely legible. Soon everything was covered in a sticky film—table top, knives, screen door handle, the phone itself. We had to watch our step as we moved between the worktable where I stripped and cut, and the stove where Mother Douglas stirred the great jamming kettle to a boil.

But that was yesterday. Today with the cleanup nearly complete, my thoughts returned to my distress at still feeling like an outsider. When we had a chance to talk, Don patiently answered my questions, but in the evenings he often went to Papa and Mother Douglas's house to study the market reports or plan the next day's work. I settled into my thoughts as I finished up kitchen chores, read Anne a bedtime story, and tucked her into her crib. I missed being in on things, even though I had no background or experience with the pressures and ups and downs of business. My dad, and then Don and I, had always been on salary.

One evening, at nearly ten o'clock, while I was finishing up the supper dishes with Mother Douglas's help, Papa and Don talked crop plans for the next spring.

"Soybeans sound interesting," Don offered. Papa sat scribbling on the envelope before him; he made no sign of having heard Don. A little later I heard Don's voice again.

"I keep hearing about soybeans, Dad—they are featured in your new copy of . . ."

"We don't need new crops, Son. Now corn . . . ," and his voice went on and on.

I was new. I was ignorant of farming, but I had been raised to believe that discussion should be used to settle differences of opinion. What I saw here bothered me. Papa Douglas was like a steamroller crushing Don's ideas and suggestions under the weight of his determination to continue in the familiar ways. I knew Don was eager to introduce soil conservation practices to prevent wind erosion. He was studying to keep abreast of new methods, and I wanted him to at least have his say. Now Mother Douglas and I heard him cheerfully agree to Papa's plans and then try once more, with enthusiasm in his voice.

"How about taking that small field we had in seed corn this year for an experiment with soybeans, Papa?"

"Plenty of time for experiments later. Let's get something on the table before we get into experiments."

I couldn't keep still any longer. Firmly hanging up my dishcloth I said, "I wish you'd listen to Don once, Papa. He's trying to help, you know!"

I didn't wait for an answer, but left the room and made my way to bed. I was exhausted, but I did not sleep. I lay there chiding myself for my brashness. I realized anew that this farming venture meant many kinds of challenges for Don, and I did not want to be on the problem side of the ledger.

Surprisingly, when Don came to bed and I tried to find

words to apologize, he responded, "He'll come around to soybeans when he sees there's money to be made. Not this year, though, it sounds like."

"But I'm talking about what I said. I'm sorry I interfered."

"Oh, he deserved that. Don't let it bother you. That's just the way he is."

Later, when I understood the family dynamics better, I suspected that Mother Douglas always made her suggestions to Papa in private. That protected his image as manager. I also understood that the three of them shielded me from financial anxieties when they could. Our joining the enterprise had not provided a magic solution to all the money problems. Also, we were becoming more deeply involved all the time, forgoing all but a bare living from the farm income and investing time and effort in plans for future projects here. Perhaps it was this realization that kept flooding my mind with disturbing thoughts—which I tried to push away, for their solution was not in my hands.

In the meantime, my city background at times loomed as a barrier to some people and at other times gave cause for sympathy, because I was now a lowly farmer. Farm or town was all the same to me. I believed my tolerant parents had raised me without prejudice, and my social work had reinforced the view that people should be valued for what they are, not for labels. I must confess, though, to one strong bias. I fully expected that when our child, granddaughter of the professor and the librarian, reached school, she would forge at once to the head of her class.

The skies brightened one day when Dorothybelle, wife

of the doctor, and Abigail, wife of the International Harvester dealer in Appleton, called on me. By a surprising coincidence, they were alums, as I was, of University High School in Minneapolis. We had an exhilarating nostalgia session, and they invited me to join the Town Bridge Club. Thereafter once a month I tasted the delights of "society." It was a pleasure, while I was struggling to find my identity as wife of a farmer, to be with friends who kept up on the latest books and drove to the cities for plays and music. For the first time since our move, I felt at home.

Big-hearted Abigail, daughter of the founder of 4-H in Minnesota, seemed to know everyone and used her home-economics training in expansive entertaining. Bright, diminutive Dorothybelle had begun practice as a physician, then retreated from small-town gender preju-

Appleton, mid-1940s

dice and left the honors to her capable husband. She specialized instead in keeping her lovely home lively with enjoyment of the arts and literature. Basking in their introduction to Appleton society, I sometimes let my imagination wander, as I pictured myself the town matron rushing to Montevideo for a new dress for the club dance. Something in larkspur blue with a full skirt, maybe. Then I'd see myself as advising on the library committee with Millie, the musical one. Or perhaps I'd be joining Abigail in getting serious about bridge, or dropping in with my sparkling toddler at Teddie's for afternoon coffee.

They often invited me to their gatherings, but the farm had to come first, and there was never time for everything. Oddly enough, I now felt somehow disloyal as my imagination roved in self-indulgent daydreams. On that first day at bridge club, something happened that made me realize how confused my feelings were. The talk turned to the sought-after roles for the school play. One contender was referred to as "that big farm kid from up north of town somewhere." The tone of voice was disparaging. Suddenly this unknown child was important to me, wherever he came from, and I felt unaccountably defensive. Whose side was I on anyway?

It was no different at church. A few rows ahead of me, I had noticed June, a husky young mother of three who, I was told, worked like a hired man on her husband's family's dairy farm. Yet she still managed to get her children to Sunday school every week. Her hands looked chapped and work-reddened when she pulled the stocking cap off her short, unruly, dark hair. When her name had been suggested as a possible helper with the younger children, a town woman carped, "I wish she would at least wipe the milk spots off her shoes before she comes to church."

I felt outraged. This farm mother's sturdy determination to improve her children's lives could teach us all something. Why must the circle of acceptance always leave someone out? Don managed to live without drawing circles at all and had many friends in both groups. I realized I was changing, but the equation was changing, too.

I began to sense that my husband was lured to the farm by more than a feeling of obligation. Don really enjoyed using the myriad skills learned in his youth that were never demanded by his city life. That discovery was especially disconcerting to me. Was this just a two-year hitch or would I be on the farm forever? More than once I heard real appreciation—even a tinge of envy in his voice—when he spoke of a family he remembered from Iowa. Three generations of this family lived on separate but nearby farms, supporting each other by exchanging help and machinery. Don's happiness was terribly important to me. Would it turn out that he wanted to follow in his father's footsteps after all? My two worlds were at war and gave me no peace. Confused, I continued to keep my doubts and frustrations to myself.

At first, I had been stimulated by all the new challenges when I came to the farm, but my enthusiasm waned as I saw my accomplishments in canning and bread making fade to mindless monotony. Seldom did I worry any more about not being able to keep up with my duties. Instead, I had a nagging feeling of being a small cog in the machinery. What did my work count for, anyway? I was just running in place, really—doing nothing more than feeding the family. I was a working part of the family but not of the community. Was I accomplishing more with my life when I helped a blind man in Manhattan find a job and hope again? Or when I located a first-floor apartment for a cardiac patient who was then able to continue to work and hold her family together?

Still, as I stood in the cool, dark fruit cellar, I should have been cheered by seeing the profusion of the garden captured in those rows of jars. Instead, I felt like kitchen help compared with Mother Douglas, who grasped all the intricacies and contributed knowledgeably to the men's plans for farm programs. I was still a hybrid—no longer a city girl, yet not really at home with farming. Would I ever be, I brooded? How strange, really, to find myself approaching mid-life in an occupation that demanded nothing of me intellectually. It offered me no promise of realizing any potential as an adult. I felt I was on a treadmill—my future captive to Papa Douglas's whim. And where did Don really stand?

I believed he was pulled one way by his loyalty to his parents and another by our early dreams, his college training, and life in the city. How much would his eventual choice be influenced by the fluctuating hope of real financial success here? Without further career ambitions of my own, I now saw myself helping Don to find his vocation and set goals.

To be honest, I never really believed he would decide to be a farmer, but I remembered that he was almost embarrassed by his success as a contact man for the Soil Conservation Service. When he was first hired, the project was at a standstill, because no one could be persuaded to try the new ways. The supervisor wanted 50 percent of the area's farms to be signed up for the program so that results could be compared. Don was told to "go in there and get all the farmers you can." Unlike other employees of the program, Don didn't call meetings and use the telephone. He went to the farms, studied the farmers' ways, shared his experience and ideas. In a short time, over 90 percent of the farmers signed up for planting in strips or on the contour. Perhaps his place was here after all, I thought, and mine beside him. Somehow, I would have to find common interests with my neighbors.

The unmistakable rumble of a tractor in the yard surprised me from my wavering misgivings. As I moved up the stairs, my new role of farm woman slipped over me again, numbing my mind and leaving only my hands and feet alive and moving.

Four-and-Twenty Thousand Blackbirds

I hate to tell you this." Don's frame filled the kitchen doorway. He threw down his dusty cap, pulled a red bandanna from his pocket, and wiped his forehead, white where it was protected from the sun.

Now what! I wondered. Would I ever learn to take the upsets of a farm day in stride? Two years ago when we lived in the city, my time had mostly been taken up by one baby girl. Now I was always out of breath trying to keep the firm schedule we had all agreed upon. I could feel Don's eyes on my face.

"The blackbirds are back."

I made an effort not to frown. It was a bright October day, and I had just finished hanging out the two-family wash. While I poured his midmorning coffee, Don pulled a chair up to the kitchen table and helped himself generously to the dwindling batch of cinnamon rolls. I reminded myself that I must start fresh bread and rolls before noon dinner. Annoyed at his news, I moved to the north window and gazed across the highway where Don had been checking our four hundred acres of golden corn still hidden in its rustling husks.

With harvest near, we might have to watch helplessly as

blackbirds by the thousands darkened these cornfields. The year before they had torn open the tips of the ears and pecked away the kernels, sometimes halfway down the ear. Just yesterday, Don joked that he'd sighted the blackbird scouts, "simply busting to get back to the flock and signal that the Douglases' corn was ripe to fatten them up for migration."

I turned and looked at him. He seemed so patient and tireless.

"You're never bitter or upset," I said, "even when they mess up a quarter of your beautiful crop. I think it's a shame!"

Don's quick smile flashed, and a loving look lingered in his eyes. "I guess you take it like it comes, Dear. What else?"

His voice was gentle. He knew that my inexperience made many things that were ordinary for him galling for me.

This spring, for example, gorgeous ring-necked pheasants and their hens strutted along the rows and, in a couple of places, picked out every seed. He had reseeded with a small hand planter, and the field now looked perfect to me. But blackbirds were harder to defeat. Scarecrows or shiny wind-driven reflectors failed to scare them away. Even timed explosive devices were of limited value. They would come, and the only possible benefit from their visit was enrichment of the soil caused by their droppings. It was hard to keep my enthusiasm up over so slight an asset. Especially on wash days. On wash days, I didn't want to think about blackbirds at all.

Frequently by the time the sun and wind had dried the clothes, some were already decorated with the blackbirds' characteristic splotches. Sheets, white clothes, and diapers had been laboriously coaxed to pristine whiteness in the huge copper boiler heated by the summer kitchen's wood stove. Mother Douglas, showing perspiration around the edge of her frilled morning cap, never lost her poise and good humor as she presided over the old Easy washer and wringers. Meanwhile, I dashed in and out of the steamy room, lugging the unwieldy basket, and struggled to pin the clothes securely on the line. The wind, ever present in the flat country, whipped and tugged at them and at me.

On that busy, sunny Monday of the blackbirds' return, a large washing already snapped and flapped. A steady wind held it horizontal—a perfect target. As I absent-mindedly sipped a cup of the strong fragrant coffee, I felt a housewifely surge of pride in the fresh supply of clean clothes spread in the sunshine. If the birds flew over our lines, however, I didn't know how I would find time to re-wash the spotted garments. Just then a dense black flock rose from the field and moved toward us.

"They must have gorged themselves already," I lamented. "Here they come."

This time Don grabbed his shotgun from over the door. We rushed outside together to try to shoo them away. The birds swirled in low over the trees in the lovely fluid way that always excites my admiration. Even as I yelled and waved a towel, I wondered what mysterious threads of sound or sight keep rapidly flying birds from touching one another as flight configurations change. Today I wanted only to get them as far away from my clean clothes as possible. Seeing us, they wavered. Then, as two shotgun blasts jarred the air, they soared like a fine billowing net that arced raggedly toward the grove. Subtly they transformed themselves into a solid tapering line, merging into the trees and virtually disappearing among the leaves.

Don leaned down to gather up several birds from the ground, and something in his manner made me hesitate before hurrying back inside to start my bread. He darted a look at me, then gazed stricken at the once-immaculate wash. My glance followed his. I couldn't believe what I saw. Spatters and spots of bright blood dotted the garments like spilled red paint.

On the farm one accepts reality. I must immediately wash out the stains. Full of remorse, Don helped me gather the soiled garments. Bread making would have to wait till tomorrow. Instead, "store-bought" bread from the supply in the freezer would accompany supper. Suddenly I realized my first thought had been of food, and I laughed aloud.

"Maybe I'm going to make it as a farmwife after all," I bragged in answer to Don's questioning look. "Neither rain nor sleet nor dark of night nor blackbirds on washday shall upset the Douglas Farm Meal Schedule!"

That day my farmer went back to his already partly denuded cornfields chuckling. I felt a stubborn pride when later I was able to serve dinner to him and Anne at twelve o'clock sharp in spite of the blackbirds. My role in the Douglas scheme of things was small, but at least I was learning to fulfill it.

Harvest of War Prisoners

Once we had made the move to the farm in 1943, with the draft board's approval, and settled into the unfamiliar routines, I had been able to keep the ugliness of the Second World War II at the back of my mind. Two summers later, however, all that was changed. In the middle of haying, John—one of the older hired hands—left for higher wages. He was not very energetic, but that was hard to find when so many young men were in the service. We had kept this hired man through the winter to be sure of having someone to count on for the crop season. When we were unable to find a substitute for him, Don had to work early and late, more than he could sustain.

As the hot days and weeks followed, I kept wondering when the war would end and we could find help for Don and return to a more normal life. When that happened, I had heard, the town fathers planned to rename the streets of Appleton as memorials to our boys who had already died in Europe and the Pacific. There was still a steady barrage of stories about the ferocity of the German people under Hitler. We presumed it was partly propaganda to bolster the war effort, but surely it must be based on something. Could there be truth to the dreadful tales of atrocities?

Don steadfastly refused to believe the rumors, saying, "They're just people like us, trying to get along in the world." But for me war was madness. Would I or my child someday have to lose a brother, husband, or son to war? Tucking Anne in for her afternoon nap, I gave her a lingering hug, rejoicing that she would never be called upon to carry a gun.

Resolutely, I put these unsettling thoughts out of my mind and hurried to make bread. I had just shaped six shiny, yeasty-smelling loaves when Don strode into the kitchen and grabbed the phone. He sank gratefully onto the chair, mystifying me with a brighter-than-usual smile. I knew he was bone weary. He had managed to cut and bale three hundred acres of the best upland hay—bluestem, redtop, and bluegrass. Because he'd had no helper to do the stacking as he ran the baler, the oblong, sixty-five-pound bales of prime hay were left lying in the large field. Now ominous black clouds, gathering in the west, threatened this important feed crop.

I spread a faded blue tea towel over the loaves where the sunshine would help them rise, and I listened in growing bewilderment to his conversation.

"Am I talking to the officer in charge?" he asked. "Can you send me twenty of the prisoners tomorrow to stack hay bales—probably two days' work? I'll pay four dollars per man. By eight o'clock? And you'll send a guard? And their food also? Sounds okay to me—tomorrow then."

"What in the world? What prisoners?" I gasped as soon as he put the phone down.

"The mailman gave me the idea," Don gloated. "Can

you believe it? There are German prisoners of war in a temporary camp at Ortonville—just twenty miles away. We didn't see it the day I drove you over there to Big Stone Lake. I'd never even heard of it. But they hire out the men to farms around here. I plan to get Bill Ahrens over to interpret. I'll put a skid on the other tractor. Twenty prisoners as farm hands! We're all set."

This is farming? I thought. I knew about Germans. Growing up, I had been told how popular my father's university classes in the German language had been before World War I. Then few people dared study German. He had become an economist and also volunteered as a government "Dollar a Year Man," scanning German-American periodicals for any hint of disloyalty or subversion. And in this war, while the fear of German Americans was lessened, the new weapons of war made the carnage unspeakable. All the hate talk came into focus. Mental pictures crowded back of butchered bodies on bloody battle fields. Headlines had screamed, "Air Raid Kills 1,500 Civilians," "Barbarous Bombing," "Polish City in Flames." Spy posters of helmeted Germans with cat eyes warned: "HE'S WATCHING YOU." I still carried a feeling of shock from a small item I'd read in the newspaper the year we moved to the farm. Apparently, a member of the President Roosevelt's own party condoned anti-Semitism on the floor of the House and was not rebuked for it. While I seldom had time for the newspaper since coming to the farm, I still wondered at the power of prejudice, never guessing it would lead to the horrors of the Holocaust.

As everyone else was caught up in the tide of hatred and fear, I, too, felt myself shrink from having anything

to do with the Germans. But no matter where my politi-
cal thoughts took me, in farming I had learned to ask
practical questions first. "Will they come to the house to
eat? What time?" I asked Don.

My anxiety must have showed, for he pulled me down
onto his lap. "For once, you don't have to think of food.
The camp will send it along."

"Coffee?" I asked, noticing that his usual high color
came back to his cheeks, smooth now since their annual
peeling from sun and wind. I smiled as he pushed his
fingers through his thick brown hair. I wished I'd known
him when he'd been nicknamed Curly—the president of
his high school class, a star in football, track, and Glee
Club.

"The camp manager says that everything is supplied.
Just relax. When have I had a chance to say that to you before? Not since we moved to the farm," Don laughed.
"Enjoy it while you can. It will all work out," he said and
kissed me.

Somewhat reassured, I said, "If only we'd get two more
days of good weather before that storm hits."

After I mentioned the weather, there was no hope of
getting more information about the prisoners. He gave
me a quick hug and hurried out with an anxious look at
the darkening western sky.

As I set about cleaning up the kitchen, I could not get
the German prisoners out of my mind. A temporary
prisoner-of-war camp near Big Stone Lake, Don had said.
If I had my geography right, this lake drained south into
the Minnesota River. Thus the lake water joined little
Pomme de Terre River, which looped through our pasture a mile south of the buildings. Men who had perhaps

killed our own boys were living in custody that close to us. Too close, I thought. How could Don be so calm about them, and even plan to use them here!

Promptly at eight o'clock the next morning, the German prisoners arrived in a big pickup truck and were marched off to the west field in their rumpled, ill-fitting work clothes. I studied them from our kitchen window. They had none of the hangdog, discouraged look that I expected. Their youthfulness also surprised me. With a spring in their step, two led the way. Many were looking around curiously, as if taking mental note of an American stock farm. The guard's eyes darted about, his gun ready. He seemed out of place—and yet reassuring. These were German soldiers, after all.

Mother Douglas came up the lane to enjoy morning coffee with me. She was happily feeding applesauce to Anne when Don hurried in to report on the workers' progress. He said he had taken a look at the small amount of cheese, bread, and water provided for the noon meal and was appalled. "The guard argued when I told him to give the men this food at ten o'clock," Don said. "He told me those weren't his orders, but I said: 'They're working for me now, and it's backbreaking work stacking those bales. They need plenty to eat.'" Don turned to me. "Can we rustle up some sandwiches for their dinner?"

Remembering his promise, I grinned and said nothing. He shrugged his shoulders helplessly, and I had to laugh. I was learning fast that everything on a farm revolves around food.

"Good for you, Son. We'll manage something," Mother Douglas reassured him. She smiled and glanced curiously at me, but said nothing more. Soon we were both busy preparing two big pork roasts for the oven. Her patrician face grew pink with her effort. Her cheerful energy and resourcefulness were never exhausted, and she had Don's easy way of making the best of whatever happened.

Later, Don told me that he had bought cigarettes, and the men were delighted when he gave them each a pack at morning break. They sat or sprawled in the sweet-smelling hay. Many of them spoke fairly adequate English, though with a heavy guttural accent. They began to ask questions about the cost of machinery and land. A blond young man ventured that he would like to return to this country after the war was over. Several nodded in agreement.

A slight fellow, hardly more than a boy, said shyly, "The Americans, they sent Karl to work in town. For a mechanic. I was helper. We got wages. I learned and saved."

Afterwards Don wondered whether they were perhaps better fed and housed in the converted youth camps here than in Germany. We knew nothing of their former army conditions. Don had learned that the camps provided showers and recreation rooms, small libraries, and playing fields. There were even musical instruments, and some did wood carving. The men appeared to be in good health.

At noon he and Papa drove the pickup to the field with our lunch—hearty sandwiches of homemade bread with thick crusty slabs of the meat. We put in baskets of tomatoes with salt shakers, lots of coffee, and hot apple pie sweetened with Karo syrup—our wartime sugar substitute. The meal was a treat to the men, and they showed their appreciation by working faster than anyone would have expected.

The rows of finished haystacks grew slowly but steadily, and Don and Bill Ahrens covered them with sheets of neoprene and tied them down with rope. The clouds hung heavy in the sky, and the shirts of the men showed dark patches of sweat in the sultry heat. Don began to believe he had a chance to save most of the crop. Well over half of the field was finished when the huge Minneapolis-Moline tractor stopped abruptly. The men gathered around it. A small part in the carburetor had broken. Don made the familiar dash to town for a replacement, but he returned half an hour later to report that the part was unavailable. They would simply have to give up any idea of finishing today and continue to do the best they could with the big old International Harvester M.

The man called Karl stepped up and looked closely at the broken part. "A piece of sheet metal you have got?" he asked. "And a coarse file? A few minutes only I need. That old part, it cannot be fixed. But a new one, that is easy."

He and Don hurried to the shop building crowded with tools and broken parts. Karl had been silent when some of the younger men had asked questions, but now as he worked he kept glancing at Don.

Suddenly he burst out, "I suppose you hate us?"

"Well, now, I don't know how you get into the army over there," Don began.

"A card to us is sent. It says, 'Come!'"

"Same here," Don replied. "Then they give us a gun and issue some ammo, and we go and shoot at each other."

Karl gave him a look that Don found to be at once searching and full of gratitude. They completed the work in what had become a comfortable, companionable silence. When the two men returned to the field, no one was surprised that the tractor part fit perfectly.

With only a quick afternoon stop for more sandwiches, fresh doughnuts, and coffee, the men finished what Don had thought would be two days' work. Don continued covering stacks until, when he came in for a warmed-over supper at ten, he could say the job was literally all wrapped up.

The storm broke noisily about midnight and woke us. Nearly three inches of rain soaked into the thirsty fields, but our precious hay crop was safe and reasonably dry.

We never saw these men again. The Ortonville camp closed in September, and the prisoners were probably moved to the main camp in Algona, Iowa, before their return to Germany. Did any of them ever follow their dream and come back to our shores? We have often wondered. Although Don had offered to give them what help he could should they return, we heard nothing. Wherever they are, I hope they sometimes have warm memories of that day.

Next morning the sun sparkled on the wet fields. I drank in the pervasive peace that follows a storm. My anxieties had been washed away.

Anne Gains a Brother and a Friend

In 1945, when Anne was three, she started Sunday school. Don and I began seeing a lot more of our new acquaintances, Herb and Donna Opp, who were also parents of a youngster there. They had met on the agriculture campus at the University of Minnesota. Now they had a large-scale hog-raising enterprise on a rich productive farm fifteen miles north of town, which his German grandfather had homesteaded nearly sixty years before. Herb and Donna were already teaching at the church when Anne entered Sunday school. Donna came to it naturally, as her mother, Marjorie Schoen, had been an early mover in the formation of the United Theological Seminary in New Brighton. Donna continued that tradition by focusing her creative energies in our small church. She and Herb collected books for a library for parents and teachers.

Reuben and Marcella Lundgren, who were also members of the church, brought an infectious sense of fun with them. Slowly, several of us women began forming a close group. There was Polly, the lawyer's wife, along with Margie and Barbara, who farmed with their husbands. The women's group also included Katherine, who led

On the Douglases' back stoop: Polly Bennett, Marjorie Erickson, Marjorie Douglas, and Barbara Kerr. Donna Opp took the picture.

the choir, Jeanette, the wife of the town photographer, and Marcella, Donna, and me. We often met with our husbands after church for a picnic or potluck and a baseball game with the children. Friendships in church and bridge club brought my attention to a brand of human values that seemed more abiding than academic excellence.

One day, as I was reflecting on some of the values that brought me to this point in my life, I suddenly remembered a crowded bench in Medical East Clinic in New York. A blind man, his thick thatch of grizzled hair white against his dark skin, called out a greeting to me. He had recognized me by the sound of my footsteps. When he had first visited the clinic, he told me a story of grinding poverty. He had outlived his wife and one of his children. Now, he was living in a crowded flat with his daughter and her family. Where did he find his courage? How could he hold onto his gentleness of spirit? I was consumed with a feeling of guilt when I thought of the advantages that surrounded me as I grew up. I wondered what I would have made of myself in his circumstances.

Anne had always sat with us at church on Sundays. Now baby Billy was ready to take her place, and Anne was excited about the idea of being in a class all by herself. She was understandably eager for this new arena that Sunday school was providing her. For the last two months, she had had to share her comfortable position as the one and only child with a new little brother who had known how to grab the spotlight even before he was born.

The previous summer, when it was nearly time for Billy's birth, Don had driven Anne and me to Crane

Island in Lake Minnetonka and left us there for a few days' vacation with my parents. They had planned to move back to town at the end of the week—well before my due date. If it occurred to us that Billy might have other ideas, we had put it out of our minds. The night before we were to move, I awoke just after midnight to strong regular contractions, but also to the worst wind and rain storm I had ever experienced. Rain was slashing in from the lake, a full ten feet across the screened porch, striking the cottage windows straight on with a rattling sound. Knowing that in the dark of this onslaught we could not cross the lake to our cars, I waited anxiously till almost dawn to waken Mother. My memory is that she leaped out of bed and landed running, at the same time chiding me in her gentle way for delaying so long. Dad readied the rowboat, which had two pairs of oars and small "kicker" outboard motor. My older brother Bob and his wife Gladys were visiting from Williamsburg, Massachusetts. I remember his carrying orange juice to each of us as if our lives depended on it. We gulped coffee and toast with no pretense of sitting down at the table.

Gladys and Mom, who stayed behind, wrapped Anne in a man's slicker and placed her on what was left of my lap as I settled on the front seat of the boat. My father and brother found that they had to ply the two sets of oars with all their strength in order to help the little engine force the boat directly into the wind. We split the waves squarely, so we were seldom splashed, but the rain continued unabated. When I caught my breath as the contractions strengthened, Anne looked at me with big eyes. Otherwise she sat quietly in the circle of my arms staring straight ahead—a funny, pathetic little figure. The collar of the big slicker had been pulled up to protect her head. Spatterings of water dripped so close in front of her eyes that, from time to time, she stuck out her tongue to catch them. We were partially protected by a big black umbrella that I managed to hold fairly steady, pointed directly into the wind.

Laboriously, we approached the south point of Eagle Island where it reached out toward Gallaher's Point on the mainland. There the wind concentrated its force as if coming through a funnel. Our sluggish progress diminished, until in spite of the men's utmost efforts, the boat was just staying in place. I closed my umbrella, and Anne and I snuggled as low as possible to cut down wind resistance. Slowly we began to forge ahead. We eased between the points and turned squarely into the bay at Zumbra Heights. The wind now hit us from the side, making progress slightly better, although the oars sometimes bit too deep or missed the water altogether as we rocked from side to side.

Finally we reached shore. Bob helped Anne and me transfer to the car. He returned to the island while Dad urged the old gray Lincoln up the steep hill. We almost despaired as we came to a large tree that had crashed down across the roadway. We found a detour, begrudging every extra minute it cost us. The twenty-five miles to town had never seemed so long. To my vast relief the obstetrician, responding to our phone call on the way, met us at Abbott Hospital.

Forty-five minutes after we had stepped through the front door, Bill entered the world on July 27, 1945, as the first grandson in either the Douglas or Myers clan. Don

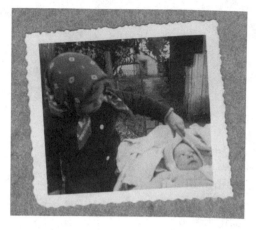

Anne and Bill, 1945

left his work in the field and reached the hospital in just over two hours, quite possibly still a record for the trip. It was a time of tender closeness and joy for us all. By the time Anne began Sunday school in September, the baby was already used to viewing the congregation from his daddy's shoulder.

On that first Sunday in the fall, Anne was exhilarated with her new adventure. As we climbed the stairs to the Sunday school room, however, her steps began to slow, and she held my hand very tightly. I signaled Don to go into the service without waiting for me. At the classroom door stood slender, competent Hazel Warren, a former kindergarten teacher and now wife of a neighboring farmer. She smiled and greeted her new student warmly. While not easily won over, Anne was stubborn in clinging to her purpose—to be in school.

Warily, she entered the beginner's room but saw to it that I took a little chair beside her. Together we enjoyed the informal atmosphere as Hazel began her lesson. She taught her own little daughter, Leslie, Anne, and four or five other preschoolers about how God provides for all the needs of each living thing in the abundant universe. Goldfish glittered in an aquarium with green plants, weeds, and snails in the bubbling water. The children began to think of themselves as God's helpers in keeping the water clean and food available. Anne, utterly enthralled, approached the container with the darting fish and appeared to have forgotten me entirely. But as soon as I made a tentative move to leave, she strongly asserted her rights.

All the following week the goldfish and the teacher figured prominently in her play and chatter. The next Sunday she entered the classroom alone, on the condition that I remain on the bench outside the door. Three times she peeked out to be sure I was still obedient to her wishes. On the third Sunday, I was dismissed at the church door to accompany Don to the sanctuary. I was beginning to learn the truth of my wise mother's words, "Once they start school, they are never yours again in quite the same way."

"The More Joy . . ."

True to my mother's predictions, Don and I learned, as all parents must, that our child was an individual. Already Anne was weaving her experiences into her own patterns of meaning. Her enthusiastic response to Hazel Warren's teachings about how the Lord provides for the needs of His creatures had surprised me. The Warrens saw the universe whole. They asked for little in material things and instead found pleasure in the world around them. They took time for fishing and observing the wild animals along the river. They did not begrudge the food or space the creatures needed, even when it meant occasional raids on the garden that provided their own food.

When Hazel told us that they were raising an orphan fawn, Anne was wildly excited. Soon after, Don needed to talk to Harry Warren about soybeans, a crop Papa now wanted to plant. I gathered up the children and we rode with Don in the pickup to the Warrens' small farm southwest of us. Two weeks earlier, Harry had been plowing a low-lying unimproved field. Watching back over his shoulder, he saw the coulter blade cut into a damp, warm hollow where he realized, too late, that a doe had recently nested. Twin fawns were hidden there. One was cut so badly it died, but Harry managed to save the uninjured one. Because he had recently seen a coyote in the area, he did not dare to leave the fawn outside to lure the mother back. Countless bottle feedings would keep this one healthy.

As we drove into the yard, four-year-old Leslie stood barefoot, silhouetted against the bright spring green. Gusty winds whipped her long brown hair around her face, as her hand rested softly on the fawn's neck. I thought of Heidi and her goats on their mountainside. The graceful fawn stayed close to Leslie but let Anne touch it timidly and briefly. When Billy saw this he would not be quiet until I stooped to let him stroke the fawn. He gurgled with delight when it licked his fingers.

Unfortunately, after harvest, the Warrens moved away and we did not know where. Their farm had made them a bare living, and I hoped they had found a better one. I missed them and thought of them one day as I prepared dinner. Before hunting season they had shut their fawn in the barn, fearing its trust of humans would make it an easy target. The game warden had stopped to remind them that it was against the law to confine a wild animal. The tearful child and the arguments of the farmer made no impression on the warden, until Harry Warren finally walked away saying, "I can't do it. If the fawn has to go, you will have to let him out." The animal's expressive eyes must have been too much for the warden. He left without opening the gate. Before their move, the Warrens had spent less and less time with the animal; it had spent more and more nights in the woods. This was only one example of their living in harmony with nature, for they had not thought of themselves as owning the fawn, but only as having befriended it.

Just then the telephone shrilly interrupted.

"Just my luck," I muttered, for I had sunk both hands into the meat loaf I was mixing. Donna Opp's welcome voice, serene and low, asked, "May I swing by and leave that child-discipline book on my way to town?" We Sunday school teachers were used to her visits on the fly.

I switched on the oven as I hurried back to my job. In what seemed like minutes, there came a crashing thump at the back door. I yanked it open to find Donna breathless, trembling, and clutching her baby boy. As I pulled her into the kitchen she sobbed, "My car. It's on the tracks. I can't move it."

Over her shoulder I saw Papa already yelling for Don as he sprinted toward the Milwaukee tracks. The railroad ran parallel to Highway 7 on the south side. There was no way in or out of the farm without crossing the tracks. And now while driveway repair was under way, rails were temporarily exposed and protruded four to six inches above the ground. Donna must have been watching for the noon flyer that was almost due and had not noticed the repair work. The front wheels had bumped over the first rail, and her car was caught fast.

I felt a rush of anger that Papa had squashed my suggestion to put a sign warning of the hazard at our driveway. He had assured us that it was not necessary for only a couple of days. That would not have been my father's way, I thought rebelliously. He would have had a warning and barriers, and probably would have left a lantern lit, besides.

I hugged Donna as she sat on the davenport quieting

the baby who, in those days before baby car seats, had been bounced to the floor but was unhurt. I'm sure the agonizing memory of the infant boy they had lost two years before intensified Donna's relief now. Self-reproach quickly replaced my blame of Papa. Why hadn't I thought to warn Donna when she phoned?

With a two-by-four the men quickly pried the car free. The noon passenger train rushed impersonally by. A chilling reverberation of its steam whistle dwindled to a distant wail. With her equanimity restored, Donna carefully made her way around the repairs and was off.

Marcella and Reuben Lundgren were younger than we, and Reub came to Don occasionally for advice while Mars and I exchanged knitting patterns and baby clothes. Their teen-age neighbor, Ginny Fairchild, attended church with them to lend her bell-like soprano voice to our choir. One Saturday, in the winter after Donna's visit, we arranged for Ginny to baby-sit so we could help out at the Lundgrens. Reuben was making the trip to the hospital in Montevideo to bring Mars and their third baby home, having left the other children with neighbors. The weather turned cloudy and colder, but we could not postpone our plans. Don and I drove over through a thickening snowfall. Then we cleaned their big white house and prepared a hearty dinner for all of us.

Late in the afternoon Reuben burst into the kitchen, his face lined with anxiety. His thin body sheltered Marcella and the new baby from a vicious wind that had turned the snowstorm threatening.

"I'll take over here. You'll have to leave right now to make it out," he ordered. "One lane has drifted shut at the big curve and the other is filling up fast." As I eagerly took the infant, Marcella removed her coat and urged us to stay.

"Don't go so soon, I wanted to tell you . . . oh, you haven't even had coffee," she began as she settled herself on the couch. "Don't you think the baby looks like Reub—her eyes, I mean?" She chattered on, scarcely taking time to draw breath. I rearranged the blankets and cuddled the tiny girl a moment before giving her back to her mother. I was flattered that they named the baby Marjorie Lynn for my mother and me.

Don was already reaching for our coats. As we left, Reuben promised, "I'll watch and bring the tractor to tow you out if need be."

We made it, and I was feeling thankful to be safe at home. Then I saw Ginny's tear-stained face, and realized how isolated and anxious she had felt. I took her in my arms.

"I was afraid for you on the highway," she confessed. "The wind sounded so fierce, and the kids were restless. I thought they might already be orphans. I didn't know what to do. The phone wouldn't even work."

In those days, I took it all for granted—Ginny's love and anxiety for my children and the many ways we all helped each other simply because there was a need.

Ginny helped us all with baby-sitting many times as we couples branched out, taking our turns as choir members, church officers, or youth group leaders. Somehow we made the projects fit around the farm work. Years later, a club of high school girls I sponsored raised money for their favorite mission of Japanese orphans by hand-gleaning ears of popcorn that our combine had missed in the field. As children in Sunday school, they had saved pennies to buy mittens for Japanese orphans who lived in a chilly airplane hangar. The horrors of war they could not imagine. Cold hands they could. One of these girls later became a medical missionary to Liberia, another a minister's wife.

Soon Anne herself was becoming a popular baby-sitter, especially for families with active boys who enjoyed having her teach them baseball skills and card games. After the children had all reached school age, we mothers stole precious hours now and then to talk about books we were reading, such as Kahlil Gibran's *The Prophet*. We discussed his words: "The deeper sorrow carves into your being, the more joy you can contain." We tried to understand.

Tragedy gave us insight. One New Year's Eve, the piercing scream of an ambulance siren sounded in the quiet countryside. Margie and her husband Fred were on their way to dinner with friends, when a drunk driver hit their car. The carnage was unspeakable. That driver, who was the father of nine, and the couple riding with Margie and Fred were killed instantly. Fred died on the way to the hospital, and Margie was so severely injured that at first we were not allowed to visit her.

Soon reports began to leak out. Once rosy and industrious, this capable woman was almost overwhelmed by physical shock. She lay pallid and languid, webbed in pulleys, tubes, and bandages. She, who had loved people and been a friend to everyone, only gradually realized the enormity of the loss of her husband and friends, as well as the damage to her own body. One cold day in January, their fine purebred Angus herd had to be auctioned off. Neighbors pitched in, however, to keep the farm operating, and her sisters shepherded her two boys.

Nurses, doctors, and family alike feared her will to live had been destroyed. But we all underestimated her. She began to yearn to be with her children. She called for friends to visit. Her shattered leg and her lacerated body began to heal, and she busied herself with plans for the farm.

We all felt a glow of pride when, after three months in the hospital, she was able to bring her family together and take responsibility again. Still limping and wearing a brace on her thigh, she returned home. She hired men to work the farm under her direction and managed well. Within a year she found time to make the weekly, twenty-mile trips to church. She often spoke of the kindness of Donald Erickson, a bachelor neighbor and longtime friend of the family who had helped during her hospitalization.

One day, about five years after the accident, Margie fairly sang an invitation: "Come for lunch at my house next Tuesday." That in itself was unusual. We seldom strayed from our kitchens at mealtime.

"What's the occasion?" we asked.

She was coy and wouldn't say. It was no one's birthday, no anniversary that we could think of. In the end we had to contain our curiosity.

Promptly at one o'clock we arrived to see Margie coming up the path from the garden, her happy face as fresh and glowing as the armful of gladiolus she carried. She could have stepped right into a wedding as she made her announcement that she and Donald would be married two weeks from that day. To our delight she invited us all to help at the church.

We all liked this quiet, steady man, and this day allowed us to share our joy for Margie and Donald. Their lives apparently blended as smoothly as their adjoining farms that were already being managed as one. We were young, and dark events quickly receded to become a muted background to our family-centered lives.

In those days, I felt the bonds of support we women developed to help one another cope with hardship. It involved the value system we tested day by day and tried to pass along to our children.

Now I think in broader terms of the interdependence of the farmers themselves, and the problems they faced and shared. Their heavier tread and the sag of their shoulders sometimes told of the frustrations these men experienced, often without complaint. But in those days, I simply accepted the gender-oriented division of responsibilities. Of course, in the back of my mind, I was aware of the corn borers that sometimes left little of our once-promising crops to harvest. I knew about the hail that shredded a field of heavy-headed wheat, cheating the combine of our best cash crop. Early rains came some years and flooded the seeds out of the ground or left sprouts rotting in shallow lakes. I thought of these setbacks in terms of consequences to the household budget and what we would be able to do for the children. It was the men who chafed and prayed for good weather and refused to be discouraged.

⌒ Taking Root

Mother Douglas and Papa, 1942

Overleaf:
Marj, Bill, Don, and Anne, late 1940s

The Awakening

The conflict began one summer day about four years after we moved to the farm. I heard a loud rumble and ran to the kitchen window, just in time to see a great cloud of dust rising beyond the fenced dooryard where the children played. I could hardly believe what I saw. Papa had dumped a truckload of lumber between the driveway and the small kitchen garden with its neat rows of vegetables and staked-up tomato plants.

What a mess. The jumble of gray, weatherbeaten boards looked rotten to me. Some had broken as they fell and would only become an eyesore there on the slope of the driveway. What possible use could they be other than to harbor little animals—maybe even rats?

Although I tried never to interfere, I was so outraged I summoned my courage and went outside to ask Papa what he was doing. To me, his answer seemed a rebuff, but apparently it was also a promise. "Oh don't worry, Marj. I'll take care of it."

While the event of the dumped lumber was new, the tension within me had been growing for a long time. Papa enjoyed joking, teasing, and telling jolly stories, but I knew what really mattered most to him—it was the business end of farming. On the other hand, he still seemed appreciative of our cleaning and enlarging the yard and planting flowers. When Don and I joined efforts with Mother Douglas to beautify the place, we no longer found pieces of wire and machinery on the ground. We all rejoiced in the slow but real progress we were making—or so I thought.

Don and I talked of enjoying soft summer evenings on our front porch, shaded by one of the largest spreading cottonwood trees we had ever seen. We kept the wide expanse of front lawn mowed, too, and planted young dwarf fruit trees along the lane fence. We had to water them by carrying countless buckets the long way around the house from the well. Hard as we worked, we could not keep the trees alive, and an extended dry spell one season killed them.

Truth was, we rarely used the front porch—the place where we had imagined relaxing and enjoying a juicy plum or cold drink. All the activity of the farm bustled around the back end of the house—via our kitchen door—and we prided ourselves on keeping that area especially tidy and uncluttered. And now, Papa had spoiled everything.

At the same time, a pile of outworn implements and machine parts grew near the shop, out of sight of the house. Papa kept saying the pile might be a handy source for repair parts, but Don knew many of the pieces were useless and tried to get Papa to call the junk man. Don, like me, wanted to reduce debris that might endanger the children.

Anne happily accepted the enclosed yard with its tall swing and canopied sandbox, but Billy treated fences as a challenge. He risked his neck trying to climb over the unstable stock gate. Whenever a gate was opened, he pushed through it to greet any visitor with a hug around the knees and "I love you." He also discovered that, like a piglet, he could squeeze under the gate near the front part of the yard and vanish from my sight. For a child so active and curious the only protection was to make the farm as safe as possible. I could imagine him trying to climb this rickety mound of boards.

What was Papa thinking of? I asked Don. He said it was just temporary—that Papa would soon haul the pile away. Day after day I waited. When it came time to cut the grass, the lumber was in the way. I remembered Papa's promise, "Don't worry, Marj. I'll take care of it." Grass-cutting time came again and again. Finally, I had to take my turn entertaining the Town Bridge Club—despite the messy driveway. I did what I could with the house to counteract the slovenly impression that unsightly clutter made. Was my new home never to approach city standards?

Day after day I studied the offending lumber pile from my kitchen window. I could not avoid it when I went to the pump. I passed it when I left for town. It began to dominate my thoughts. As my irritation increased, that ugly pile started to symbolize all the frustrations of my life on the farm: the constant work never finished, not enough time with the children, being out of touch with old friends and my family, the feeling of not being really in charge.

Dreaming one night, I saw Papa's powerful figure standing on top of the stack of lumber, his huge scornful face bobbing above me as he looked down on my shrunken self in the driveway. It was like the child's game of "I'm the king of the castle, and you're the dirty rascal"—and I knew which one I was. I could not rid myself of this belittling message. Finally, I resolved to talk again with Papa.

Once I had made up my mind, it took a long time to find the right opportunity to question him. Then late one fall morning, as I hurried home from errands in town, my mind racing ahead with plans for the noon dinner, I spied him coming up the lane. This was my chance. I hailed him, and, as he turned to come toward me, I rushed inside to empty my arms of groceries. As I hoisted a sack to the table, it split and packages spilled out.

"Wouldn't you know it! Just like all the rest of the morning," I panted. After a late start I had stopped at the church to leave a cake for an afternoon funeral. The minister had intercepted me and complained to me again about the ill-prepared new Sunday school teacher. When I had managed to get away and on to my next errand, the blacksmith hadn't had the piece of machinery ready for me to pick up for Don. Then Miller's store had not had the frozen peaches I needed for a dessert, and that meant one more stop.

Thinking things couldn't get any worse, I left the spilled groceries on the table and hurried back outside. Papa had reached my steps.

"The busy housewife!" he greeted me with a half-smile.

The shadow of his old felt hat fell across his face, and his gray denim work jacket hung crooked on his sturdy figure. Its big patch pocket was overstuffed as usual, probably with correspondence about his inventions.

"It's been a busy morning all right. Everything went

wrong—and then I drove in past that messy pile of lumber. What possible use is that, Papa? You've never used any of it, have you? You said you'd take care of it. When, Papa, when will you get rid of it?"

He smiled in an indulgent, superior way as we faced each other there on the steps. He was so maddeningly unreachable. Aware of *only* what he wanted. His face seemed to hang over me as it had in the dream.

And then his answer came: "Oh, Marj. It's okay there. It may come in handy someday."

His reply struck me like a blow. It was an insult. Didn't I count for anything? All these weeks I'd believed he was planning to move it. Now I realized he never meant to. He had deceived me.

My frustration closed in like a blank wall. Fury took over. Before I knew what was happening, my body tensed and my right arm flew into the air. I heard the crack as my hand smacked his firm cheek.

I, who always felt there was a peaceful way to handle anything, who never spanked the children, who tried to train the dog with love pats—I had slapped Papa! It was not a hard slap. Something slowed me before my hand touched his cheek, but I heard the sharp sound and saw his eyes startle wide. He said nothing. Nor did I. I turned and ran into the house and curled up on the couch crying, shaking with anger and shame. Don met Papa in the barn and came in to find me weeping and staring at the hand that still stung from Papa's starting whiskers. I'm sure he wondered, as I still do, how I could have reacted in such a shocking way, but he took me gently in his arms.

"It's been hard for you, I know." He soothed me as I spent my anger in unaccustomed tears. As he held me, I could tell he was miserable to see me this unhappy, but as usual his words were few.

Then he surprised me by saying, "Dad's not easy for anyone—even Mother—though she's managed to establish some rights, and he knows he has to respect them." He said no more, and I could only guess at his meaning. I knew he had been deeply hurt when, as a boy, his father punished him—more than once—and refused to believe his innocence in some neighborhood prank. Don was proud of his father's business ability, but they had never been as close as he and his mother were. When we moved here, I had been determined to get along with Papa at all costs. Now what had I done but make things more difficult for Don?

"I'm afraid I'm just blaming him for everything, Don. He didn't seem to care what we gave up to come to the farm—as long as we came."

"I know—he's that way."

"And then we tried so hard to make it nice here—and he didn't want us to waste our time planting those trees."

"That's right—or our money."

"And he wouldn't even consider soybeans when you suggested them."

"No, he likes to be the idea man."

"And then that darned lumber pile. Why does he do a thing like that?"

"Why is he Papa? It's just the way he is, Marj. If it's all too much . . . ?"

"Oh no, Don. You know better. You were certainly patient in giving me my time at social work. Nothing's changed. You know I'm behind you all the way. It has to be your decision. I'm afraid I've tried to keep all my dissatisfactions inside until they boiled over. I hope he doesn't blame you."

"I have the feeling that lumber pile will disappear," Don comforted me. Then, the fun back in his voice, he teased, "I'm pretty sure you got his attention—and that's a start!"

"I'm glad if I did, Don. It's important to me to have our place look decent. If he and I are going to live together, he's got to know there are some things I care about, too."

Nothing was ever said again about the incident, but Don was right. Papa burned the woodpile, and in the wet year that followed, the grass grew back. We were able to mow and trim the driveway again. As far as I know, Papa said nothing about the expense when Don and I re-planted a couple of Dolgo crabapple trees. He took pains to comment on the incomparable jelly Mother Douglas and I later made from those crabs each fall. Sometimes at our frequent meals together, he gazed silently at me and apparently listened as Mother and I chatted about the buckthorn hedge and how it attracted cedar waxwings. Eventually, he let Don call the junkman to carry off the old implements and machinery—except for the few things he took back at the last minute, for they might "come handy," as he put it. Perhaps the thing that brought us together again was his pride in his new grand-son; he called him the "child with the noble head." Grad-ually our relationship mellowed into something akin to appreciation. I believe it was important that I had come closer to knowing who I was and to being more able to state my needs.

And I admit I still smile when I think of the lovely blaze that lumber pile made.

Anne on King, several years after her sixth birthday

Come and Bring Your Pony

Now that Anne was in school, she longed to have her new friends visit the farm. By the time of her late October birthday, her constant chatter about the pony King had made him famous in the Appleton first-grade room.

"Why not let her have a pony party?" Don suggested. "The kids could all have rides."

"Yes, yes, yes!" Anne jumped out of her chair and grabbed her daddy around the neck in her excitement.

"With only six guests for six years old!" I hastened to remind her.

From the day a year ago when this shaggy Shetland first joined our family, Don had taught Anne to feed and water him and how to handle the saddle and harness. She tried in vain to teach King to hold his head high as would a king, but in this, he was stubborn and usually kept a weary and plodding look.

I gave no further thought to entertainment. I was delighted to leave that part of the fun to Don and Anne.

If only my luck had held! On the day of the party the hired man was called home at noon for an emergency, and Don, of course, had to take his place at the corn picking. I was aghast. I would have to cope with party and pony by myself.

As the children hopped off the school bus with happy anticipation, I counted only four guests.

"The others have ponies," Anne announced happily, and added, "so I told them just to ride on over."

I barely checked the words, "You should have asked." At this stage chiding would not change anything. But three ponies! It was not reassuring to remember that Patty was one of the missing guests. I knew that she, along with her sister, practiced being cowboys by jumping from the hayloft loading-window to the back of their brindle cow as it emerged from the barn door below. I wondered what games Patty might concoct today?

The other pony owner, Tim, was a little boy from a farm north of town somewhere; I couldn't bear to think what his talents might be.

Horses completely baffled me. I had grown up with a tennis racket in my hand, and swimming was second nature, but horses remained a mystery. When King once went out of his way to scrape Anne's leg against the metal gatepost, I thought it was accidental, but I was soon disillusioned. We all learned to be on guard for such mischief when he had been ridden longer than usual.

Tim soon turned up on a chestnut pony that at first was as skittish and shy as Tim. Luckily Patty came in sight right behind him. She ignored the stirrups, which swung loose, but I rejoiced that she had not come bareback.

Just then King appeared at the door of the barn. He was resplendent in a spangled harness and stirrups my parents had found in Mexico for Anne's birthday. He saw the ponies and tugged at the reins, which were held by three children each trying to lead him. Anne stopped the procession and, as she had been taught, retightened the cinch. Patty quickly slid off her pony to help her. As the group converged, Billy and I joined them to welcome Patty, meet Tim, and get acquainted with the new ponies, Speed and Trigger.

We established "turns" and got three guests mounted, each with the owner as attendant. They all reluctantly agreed there would be no racing, but, in spite of this, the activity in the driveway circle was soon dizzying to watch. At first I busied myself keeping the children who were on foot out of the way of the riders, but they all wanted to be together and were soon running alongside.

The weather was crisp, and the warmth of the late afternoon sun was welcome on my shoulders. This day was not going at all as I had planned. Don's parents and brother Glenn, Glenn's wife Lillian, and their two girls were coming for a meal after this party. I still had a lot to do.

My thoughts turned nervously to unfinished tasks for supper. From where I stood I could see the tomatoes intended for the salad still on the vines. By this time the sweet potatoes should have been in a casserole in the oven with the ham. I would also have to clean up after the party. When would I ever get used to days like this that just went on and on as if they had a mind of their own and ended with everything happening at once?

At least the ponies were behaving beautifully. Ponies and kids surely belong together, I observed. The children quickly learned to hold the reins properly. Even timid Helen gained confidence and now seldom reached for the comforting security of the saddle horn. On Trigger,

Jack slapped the reins and nearly lost his balance when the pony came quickly to a trot, sides sleek and shining and head up. Patty's mount pranced a little and would have run if her owner had not kept a close watch. Each child wanted repeated turns on each horse—even Patty's Trigger, who intimidated them a little. But when Billy's turn came, he would have no other. Used to quiet King, his confidence was unbounded, and he insisted on being boosted to Trigger's back. His short legs far above the stirrups struggled to get a grip on her round sides. Grabbing the reins he leaned to pet the pony's neck and talk to her. She turned her head to roll her eye at him and obediently began to walk. He relaxed comfortably in the saddle, and Patty took my place walking him round and round.

As we watched, the guest ponies came around the little shop building from opposite directions. King, as usual, was lazing along near the barn, and Tim was tugging at his reins trying in vain to make him run. The others, in contrast, were both trotting, and two town children, Jack on Trigger and little Helen on Speed, were grinning and big-eyed.

Just as the ponies should have passed each other, they swerved together and suddenly reared up, front hooves pawing and their surprisingly big yellow teeth bared. Running frantically toward them, I became aware of their wildly rolling eyes. Could I get the youngsters out of the way in time? Why, oh why wasn't Don here?

Horrified, I observed that Jack had let go of the reins, which were hanging loose and flapping. Would that make the pony bolt? Helen's feet did not reach the stirrups, and she had slid to the side of the small saddle, both hands now grasping the saddle horn and knuckles white. Doggedly she hung on while, in amazement, I saw my daughter calmly step up from the back, grab the bridle, and pull one pony away. I reached Helen just in time to circle her waist with my arms, and she clung gratefully for a moment as I put her feet on the ground. Meanwhile Patty rushed up right behind Anne, and, under her familiar hand, her well-trained pony instantly turned docile. Jack slid awkwardly down and stepped away a bit unsteadily. Just then our fat King trotted up to join in, but he was too late. The "fight" was already over. It was years later that I learned from my daughter that Patty, the would-be cowboy, had purposely taught her pony to rear up on his hind legs, the trick that had started the trouble.

There were a few more rides, but the kids' hunger brought them trooping into the house. I remember Anne's face rosy with pleasure as she made her secret wish, blew out the candles, and guided the knife on the first wobbly cut in the cake.

When it was time to pile into the car for the trip back to town, there was no doubt that our "different" birthday party had been a success. As my car slowly followed the two ponies and riders out the driveway, the phrase, "Never again!" repeated itself resolutely in my mind. I suppressed a wry smile as the thought struck me that Anne's secret wish might well have been for yearly repetitions of a pony birthday party. If horses were to be a big part of the children's lives, I would have to become more expert. And, I reminded myself, I would have Anne's help. Already, at six years of age, her confidence and ability in some ways exceeded mine.

Food and Those Who Ate It

Food is the magnet around which so many of my farm memories cluster. Small wonder. Hearty food in vast quantities was needed three times a day. I remembered the obstetrician who had looked at Anne—newborn, long and slender—and said, "Babies are like empty stockings. Just fill her up." I hadn't appreciated the remark at the time, but I had been at the job of filling people up ever since.

You've heard of a "generous hand" in cooking? Well, Mother Douglas certainly had one. Her largess extended even to the pets, and items like leftover pork chops and dressing were broken up for the dogs' and cats' dishes. Under her hand, cream and butter and seasonings transformed even plain old carrots into a succulent treat. Thick sour cream and extra eggs fluffed her waffles. Long after her death, Papa would still beg me for pork hocks and noodles or small-curd cottage cheese "like Vivian used to make." I never thought I got it quite right but he apparently did.

One food I could never replicate for him was the justly famous specialty of Don's grandmother. It was known as Grandma Moats's Hot Sweet Chopped Green Tomato Piccalilli. The tomatoes had to be harvested just before the first killing frost. Then you had to collect red peppers, onions, condiments, spice bouquets, and, of course, mustard and vinegar. Even Mother Douglas did not know the complete list nor the exact proportions, because the recipe was a tightly guarded secret.

When the Douglases lived in Benson, Grandma Moats lived with them, as did her frail sister whom we called Aunt Belle. From my visits to Don's house as a college student, I remembered the two white-haired women in their dark, practical housedresses, knees spread to support the dishpans of potatoes they always seemed to be paring for dinner. I understood that Grandma Moats had sworn her sister to secrecy about the recipe.

Grandma Moats had not always been so tight-lipped, but as her delicious mix steadily gained fame at home and at church suppers, people constantly asked for it. Papa began to tease that he was going to steal the recipe, market the relish, and gain fabulous wealth. Grandma, a widow concerned about money, began to guard her secret jealously, especially from Papa (or, as time passed, from any possible spies).

Mother Douglas reminisced about the controversy one day as we sat in the sunny kitchen peeling tomatoes we had scalded for canning.

"The relish was sweet and sour, too," she began. "It was too tart for a sauce and too hot. I know there was plenty of red pepper in it. Wonderful with meat, especially pork. And a little bit went a long way. I've seen it bring tears to a grown man's eyes." She almost giggled. "We canned it in pints, and a pint lasted for days even with extra men at the table."

"But you said a whole relish dish of it disappeared?" I prompted.

"Yes. Once at threshing time the men gathered at that long harvest table we used at Benson. The men joked and laughed as they seated themselves—all except for Frank, a quiet fellow who was new to the bunch. My mother and Aunt Belle had helped all morning and I made them sit down with the men. Mother would not sit until she found a place for her precious bowl of piccalilli among the crowding trays of bread and dishes of butter, jam, and cabbage slaw. I brought platters of pork roast, mashed potatoes, baked beans, and tomatoes. In a second, the noise stopped and they all started in."

"You didn't sit down?"

"No, I had just got busy pouring coffee when I noticed a look of real distress on my mother's face. I soon discovered why. The new man had started on her dish of relish, which was near the edge of his plate, and he did not pass it on to the others. He must have assumed it was his side dish. He was eating it like a dish of applesauce, and it seemed to have no effect on him."

"I'll bet Grandma was wild! Didn't she say anything?"

"No, I was afraid she'd choke, but she kept still. He'd have been so embarrassed if he'd realized what he'd done."

Mother Douglas was laughing now, but her quick fingers worked as rapidly as ever. "Then I was afraid Frank would choke," she continued. "He was really gobbling that hot stuff—he must have been brought up to clean his plate!"

"Papa didn't notice?"

"Oh, trust him! But it was too late. Frank had laid down his spoon by an empty dish."

"Now, are you going to tell me that Frank had enough fire in his belly to do the work of two men that afternoon?"

"That's what Papa claimed—said he'd use the story in advertising. His motto would be 'Grandma Moats's Hot Sweet Chopped Green Tomato Piccalilli is energizing and safe in any amount.'"

Her story reminded me of when my friendliness had been tested by two hired men, a Mexican and an Indian, who were with us for two or three weeks. Inspired, I put my small bottle of Tabasco sauce on the table, thinking our food might seem bland. Apparently it did! I had used that same bottle from the time we were first married, measuring exactly ten drops in a celebrated salad dressing. They showered it on meat, potatoes, and vegetables, and sopped it up with bread. When I asked Don to get another bottle on the next grocery order, I told him, only half joking, "If I ever see them put that stuff on my pie, they will never come back, I mean it."

It was feeding the neighbors who came to help and the hired men, of course, that created most of the work in the kitchen. When neighbors were our helpers, there was news and friendly gossip. Sometimes they joked and told stories about the community that I enjoyed, as I waited on them and the children, snatching a bite when I could. Hired men were more a part of the farmers' world, and Don always found a basis of comradeship with his men. I tried to visit with them at meals, but mostly their talk was of the fields and machinery. Still, I remember them best through food. Sometimes I packed up iced tea in a thermos bucket and sandwiches and cake or cookies and rattled out to the field with the toy wagon. The children often trailed along, and a short picnic made a pleasant, albeit dusty, break in the day.

To this day I can't see a pork chop without thinking of Red. He was a big, powerful, good-natured bachelor from town who played in a German band all winter and lived on unemployment benefits most of the summer. Don talked him into becoming temporary crew foreman because of an unusual problem.

We had hired two young men from town after rain had delayed the cultivating. They ran the machinery well enough, but the work proceeded very slowly. Don suspected they were taking naps in the sunshine when their tractors were out of his sight, but he couldn't afford to stop his own work long enough to prove it. Their bad habit abruptly ceased when Red joined us. Coincidentally, we noticed a couple of freshly blackened eyes. The arrangement got us over the hump and is the only time I can recall when Don's relationship with his helpers needed strong-arm tactics.

Red was fond of my pork chop casserole. Thus, when he agreed to work Easter Sunday so that we could keep a long-promised dinner date at the Lundgrens', I made this favorite dish for his dinner. I browned eight large pork chops, covered them with raw rice, generous slices of raw onion, and tomatoes, and left them in a slow oven to stew. I assumed that I'd have leftovers ready for Monday. Suffice it to say that Red loved to eat, and we did not begrudge him a single pork chop.

Sometimes hired hands shared more than our food, though. They shared hopes, disappointments, and daily life.

For several years, Andy Larsen lived with his family in one of our houses. His three small children and our kids played together. One day he indicated to Don that he was trying to save to buy a little land of his own. Hearing that, we gave them garden space and paid him extra for odd jobs. During a spree one weekend, he accidently let his wife discover his secret. Once she knew, nothing would do except to turn over the savings to her to squander. Thoroughly discouraged, Andy began frequent excessive drinking bouts and sought a job in town.

The following year a lively young fellow asked Don for work so that he could be married to the daughter of a well-respected German farmer just northwest of us. Don offered to supply paint, lumber, and wallpaper for them to decorate a two-room building that had been used as an office before we came. Hank proved to be an excellent farmer and well worth the higher wages he had requested. They stayed only a year before a better job called, but our friendship has lasted.

Old Joe was different. He came to the farm one day in his old Ford pickup, with the door on the passenger side tied shut with rope. His eyesight was failing, and he assured us he never drove over fifteen miles an hour, and then only on the shoulder! We didn't really need a man at the time, but he apparently had nowhere else to go. He eagerly offered to work for us at a low wage that Don promptly raised, as Joe became both useful and trusted. We had assumed he would not handle machinery nor take much initiative. Only later we discovered, through stories he told the children, that he had once been an assistant agent on an Indian reservation and carried considerable responsibility. He proved to be easy with the stock, prompt, and reliable at chores, and he watched out for the children's safety when they followed him about. Finally we felt enough confidence to go to the Twin Cities for a long-postponed overnight with my parents, leaving Joe in charge of the farm. On our return we found that he had sold last year's hay (which he knew we didn't need) to farmers who had come by seeking some. There on the kitchen table lay the money with his careful notations.

Don could remember with fondness a hired man who had been like a member of his family and had taught him to read the newspaper before he started school. But this was my first time of sharing our daily life with a person who had no close family of his own. Joe's discharge from the agency, due to the frailties of age, must have been traumatic for him, but I never heard him talk about it. How lonely and useless he must have been feeling when he turned up at our farm seeking work. His two-year time with us met a real need for him, and he proved to be a contented, useful employee. Eventually he was welcomed into the home of a nephew in South Dakota for his final years.

Perhaps I noticed Joe's loneliness more because I could see Don's circle widening. While Papa and Mother Douglas kept a low profile, seldom even attending church, Don radiated the confidence born of his comfortable upbringing; he was liked and trusted. Often on Saturday evenings, we made popcorn and read aloud or played games with the children. Don, however, sometimes had errands or needed to visit Perry's Barber Shop. That often ended with a shared bottle, but serious drinkers went to Correll, as Appleton always voted dry.

When I occasionally served hot gingerbread with applesauce or chocolate cake and the eternal coffee for one of Don's informal committee meetings, I could see his feeling of belonging through these contacts—and not only belonging. It became clear that people sought out his opinion, people from a wider community, less stratified than the one we had known in the city. (He continually encouraged the merchants of Appleton to admit a big chain store to increase their trade area, but they feared the competition and had to watch the neighboring town of Montevideo grow and thrive instead.)

My work of preserving, preparing, and serving food remained constant, however. I always had some hired help to feed during the crop season—except for our last summer when Don offered the job of hired hand to Anne and Bill. Bill got up early and ran a tractor till noon, Anne worked from noon till late supper. Each was faithfully paid one half of full wages every Saturday night. Anne later went to college, cherishing the knowledge that her daddy had said she "could disc in a dead furrow better than he could."

Life should have been simpler for the distaff side when big machinery replaced some of the hired men and threshing rings. Food was served in much smaller quantities than in the old days—but often at strange hours. Many times when bad weather threatened, but the crop was dry and right for harvest, Don ran our big combine all night. He stopped in for hot lunches or carried sandwiches and coffee with him to keep him safely awake. I had to agree with Mother Douglas, who insisted that headlights on tractors should never have been invented. They robbed farmers of their rightful rest—to say nothing of farmers' wives.

When winter weather was severe, Don arranged with Willy, who was the International dealer and also drove the township plow, to watch for our yard light. If he found it on after a storm, he stopped and plowed us out, knowing I would have roast beef sandwiches ready and lots of hot coffee. Of course Don paid him, but it was the food, I think, that lured him to come so promptly—and it saved us hours of hard work. If the snowfall was especially heavy, Don joined his friend as he went back to plowing out the county roads. They roared through the night. While Willie guided the big blade, Don kept his eyes fastened on the sloping wingblade as it swept the roadside and yelled a warning if an obstruction loomed in the swirling whiteness.

I would snuggle back into bed, thinking of Mother Douglas again and her saying to me as a newcomer that farm people worked hard and deserved the best food and lots of it. I ruefully added to myself—yes, and apparently at all hours!

Aerial view of Douglas farm

Rustlers and Don's Coin Trick

L ook at this, Papa." Don placed his meticulous records before his father. "Theft of stock has cost us at least $2,500 in the last two years. That's hard to believe, but there it is."

They studied the figures with sober faces. Papa would never admit that he had failed to realize the extent of the problem. He knew, of course, that stock had been stolen, but he preferred to explore new sources of income rather than modify present operations. One year he spent hours scheming to figure out how to make gas for fuel from the abundant sweet clover that grew almost waist high. Although it worked, it would have been expensive to perfect and market.

The year Ford and the English Ferguson company broke up their partnership, Don bought a little Ferguson tractor, but Papa got a Ford and had the fittings reversed. He drove it backwards with the machinery in front of him. Thus he did not have to turn around to watch the rows as he cultivated or planted. One problem remained: the steering was also backwards, requiring him to remember to steer left to go right. He insisted he soon adjusted to that, but Don was not so sure when he saw the long scratch on the side of our car. Papa invented a combination field hoe and rake and tinkered with other machinery. In his later years his irrepressible urge to try things out resulted in his writing several country-style songs. He paid to have them set to music, and although they proved to be very singable, they were never marketed. He was creative and resourceful, but he lost interest if success was not immediate. He liked to "think big," not watch details. Now, with the theft loss, he would be forced to tighten up.

All four of us were cheerfully committed to working hard and plowing any profits back into the business. However, the lost money set us to dreaming of the new sofa Mother Douglas needed for their small tidy living/ dining room, the toys that the children would like for their birthdays, the trips to the Twin Cities to visit friends and my parents, the big machinery that could replace some of our hired help. The men were fiercely determined to forestall any thefts in the future. The winter passed without incident, and I began to hope the problem had passed, too.

In the spring, four hundred sheep were turned into the west pasture where, at first, they huddled together. Their backs made a lumpy wool carpet covering the center of the field. Presently, it ravelled into ragged throw rugs, gray against the green as the sheep dispersed into groups, heads down and busily cropping. Being a light sleeper, Don wakened several nights in a row hearing disturbances among the sheep. Each time he hurried through the grove to the pasture and each time found nothing. At planting time, a time-and-weather-sensitive task, Don insisted on doing it all himself. Putting in sixteen- or eighteen-hour days, he could ill afford to have the five or six hours of rest be broken by these anxious skirmishes. He began to grow preoccupied and lost his steady good humor.

Finally he belled the liveliest ewes, and the next night a sustained tinkling again aroused him. I saw him pull on his pants and shoes and slip out, grasping his rifle. He must have shivered in the chill night air. He later told us that, as he quietly stepped out of the shadows of the trees, he found the sheep clearly illuminated in brilliant moonlight. He noted with surprise that a strange truck was parked in the road ditch beyond the pasture. Amazed, he saw a boyish figure brazenly encircling a band of the sheep with snow fencing and crowding them up to the truck where he could easily hoist twenty or twenty-five of them in and drive off.

The frustrations of the nightly searches and an unaccustomed anger swept over Don, he admitted later. He swung the rifle to his shoulder and almost instinctively lined up the sights with the interloper's head. At last he had a target, and the insufficient rest and nagging worry crested in a wave of fury. He was ready to shoot to kill. Then he sobered. "I couldn't do it," he said simply. "I figured the fellow probably had his own troubles."

Instead, he released a warning bullet that carried its deadly threat close to the hatless head so plainly visible. The man threw himself into the grass. Don waited poised and hardly breathing. The sheep jostled and stirred restlessly and then huddled closer within the circle of fencing. When the figure presently rose and began to run in a crouched position, Don sent another bullet smacking into the side of the truck. That stopped the thief, but unbelievably he had the nerve to try a third time to escape in his truck. He's desperate or crazy, Don thought, and made the rifle bark again. The bells sounded briefly, then all was quiet. The man flattened himself against the ground and was invisible. Adrenalin pumping, Don kept a tense and steady watch. Finally he realized the man must have wriggled to the shelter of the ditch and crept away in the tall grass, abandoning his vehicle.

Tracing the license was easy. The fellow proved to be a recently discharged worker from the mill who had a wife and small children. Without savings, he was desperate for food for them. Obviously he was no novice at handling sheep, but he had no other record of rustling stock. This clumsy attempt was probably his first. Don enlisted the aid of the Town Board in finding work for him. Jail would have meant public support for the family, and neither he nor the township wanted that.

After the planting was finished, Don made a hasty trip to a place near Mobridge, South Dakota, where he got a good buy on fifty young feeder heifers. These he put on the river pasture. Several farmers had pastures that adjoined ours in an irregular pattern. Henry was one who always failed to take care of his half of the fencing promptly. More than once, Don made the necessary repairs to the shared fencing when Henry neglected his small half. The man was never at home to help when there was an emergency, and we guessed that he was often at the river with a fishing pole in his hand.

Fearing more theft, Don bought newly minted quarters at the bank and inserted them under the skin of the brisket on his young animals. They healed quickly and the animals fattened nicely on the plentiful, protein-rich upland hay and white clover. Apparently, Henry had more time to admire their sleek good looks than he did for his fencing duties, and he tried an old ruse. He stopped Don in the field one day to insist one of the heifers was his. Unwisely, he claimed it had "somehow got through the fence" to join Don's herd. Don explained that his stock had all been bought from one breeder and bore his brand. Henry looked a bit nonplused at that and admitted that he had no sale bill, but he stubbornly stuck to his story. Day after day he sought Don out to argue with him so noisily that Don finally summoned the "law" to call his bluff. Don saddled faithful old Ranger and led him as the three men walked to the pasture. Don kept expecting the former to back down. Instead, he grew more aggressive and unpleasant.

Stridently, Henry complained, "You guys have it easy. You don't notice one more in your herd, but I can't afford to let you keep it."

He was trying to work on the sheriff's sympathy, Don decided as he later described the scene.

"I make a head count and check for problems every week. I've got my fifty and no more."

"Fifty-one, you mean!"

"All right, point yours out!"

Although Don's horse, Ranger, was accustomed to cutting out one animal at a time, it took a while before Don on the horse and the men on foot had cornered the cow the neighbor indicated. Don said later he wondered whether Henry planned to indicate another animal and another as his lost cow until they would allow him one to get rid of him. In any case, it was time to give the man something to remember.

Don quietly handed the sheriff his pocket knife and said, "Feel here under the neck, and you'll find a coin. The coin is a quarter, and I can tell you the year it was minted. Henry, would you care to guess? No? Then cut it open, take out the coin, and try me."

Henry's mouth actually dropped open. Then he looked at Don indignantly as if he had somehow been cheated.

For a long moment, even the heifer stood silent and, like the two accusers, stared at Henry.

Then Henry's ranting and noisy swagger drained from him, and he growled, "Keep your damned heifer, then."

Abruptly he turned and started home across the pasture. Don and the sheriff watched as Henry strode angrily away, kicking at the rocks in the field. The sheriff shook his head but kept his comments to himself. The hot work of rounding up the heifer seemed at the time like wasted effort, but stealing from that source at least was never again attempted. Apparently the sheriff never told the story, and understandably, Henry did not. Among ourselves we laughed and called it "Don's Coin Trick."

We have always wished we could see the expression of the unsuspecting butcher who would some day find those coins, or hear the explanation when they turned up in a housewife's kettle of barbecued brisket.

Constables and Cornfields

Big burly Jay, whose land lay east of us, had never really had his heart in farming. He ran a business in town and finally decided to rent out his farm and live in Appleton. The renter he chose was new to the area, and we never happened to meet the man nor his workworn wife. His name was Albert, and we heard that he was young and husky but a "lazy farmer," the neighborhood decided. The place looked untidy—machinery was left in the field, and broken fencing was never repaired. Word circulated in town that Albert had a violent temper, easily triggered over a grocery bill or a refusal for credit on gasoline.

Not surprisingly, by the middle of the summer stories began to circulate that Albert and Jay argued constantly over terms of rental and payment, use of machinery, storage, fencing. In fact, they probably argued over every facet of their business together. Jay himself had a reputation for slipping out the back door of his business when he saw an unpaid creditor approaching at the front.

One day in July, Jay stopped by his farm to make use of a wagon to move a piece of furniture. It was hot, and he was in a hurry to get back to his business. When he discovered the renter had borrowed the wagon for fertilizer and left it crusted with a smelly residue, angry words turned to shouts, and a fistfight erupted. The frightened wife alerted the constable, who arrived just as the men staggered apart, both bleeding, watchful, and hostile. The constable was so intimidated by their bloodthirstiness and threats that he turned in his badge that same day.

The following morning a committee from the township called on us, and we sat down to coffee and cookies at the kitchen table while they told us the story. Apparently tales of Don's matter-of-fact courage in defending our property against theft had reached them, and they had come to ask him to act as temporary officer until they could find a new constable. Though overloaded with work, he finally reluctantly agreed.

As the group left, the town clerk asked him, "Are you scared?"

"Scared? No." Don laughed. "They've had time to think it over, and I'll bet there's not enough money in both town banks to get those two to go at their fight again."

He was right about that, but he did not realize that once the badge had found a resting place, there was not enough concern (nor ever an occasion) for anyone to seek another constable. Not until we sold the farm did Don manage to get rid of his dubious honor and the ostentatious badge, wasting its brilliance in his dresser drawer.

Don's authority as constable was useful that fall, however, when twenty or more hunters, bristling with shotguns, invaded our farm. They were taking advantage of a special hunting season set up because the deer population was getting out of hand. Don enjoyed hunting and was always generous in granting use of his land to responsible people. But it was different with a sporting, noisy bunch just out for a good time. Then, like any farmer, Don's first thought was for the safety of his stock, to say nothing of the annoyance of trampled, broken cornstalks at picking time.

Don noticed the activity in our west cornfield and junped into the pickup to go investigate. He recognized the swaggering leader as Olaf who, perhaps bolstered by a few friendly beers, was striding along in advance of the group. Don knew him as a laborer at occasional odd jobs around town.

"What is it, boys?" Don asked. "I haven't opened my land for hunting."

Don knew some of the men by sight and could identify at least two as small landholders near Olaf's place by the river. One had bought seed corn from him, another borrowed a wagon that Don had to retrieve when he needed it. They hesitated and gathered around Don, irritated at having their outing interrupted. An angry grumbling began. The hunters looked around for Olaf, who was moving quietly to the edge of the group, making himself as inconspicuous as possible. They turned on him accusingly.

Realizing he was trapped, he blustered, "The game warden said you ain't got enough 'No Hunting' signs."

"Olaf, my land has been posted ever since I've lived here. You all know that. You've all driven past those signs many times on the highway and on the county roads, too."

"Well, you ain't got enough, the game warden says, and we go by what he says. So c'mon, boys!" He swung his gun to his shoulder and made as if to lead them off.

"Hold it, Olaf! There'll be no hunting here on my land today or any other day. I'm the constable. Have you forgotten that? I'll have to run you in if you give me any trouble. And that goes for the game warden, too."

Although he was the only unarmed man among them, the resolve in his voice could not be mistaken. One by one they turned away, still protesting, and overtook Olaf, who again was trying to slip out of the way. As they pushed toward him, Don overheard one demand, "Gimme back my five bucks, you bum!"

"What five bucks?" Don demanded.

"The five bucks he collected from each of us guys to hunt here."

Don was momentarily speechless. "Olaf, you collected five dollars a head from these men to hunt my land without ever checking with me?"

"Well, here's where the deer are. They like your pasture best," he began weakly.

"And they like to feed on my cornfields, too. Last year I just raised the picker head and put the tractor in high gear when I reached the center of one field. Sorry, fellas. I've had my own troubles with those deer, but a crowd of hunters with slugs and shotguns I don't need.

"Next time ask the owner, not Olaf," Don continued. "The only hunting rights Olaf can sell are for his own land, and I'll back him all the way on that. Now you'll have to settle your own score with him."

By the time Don returned to the house to tell me about Olaf's boldness, he was laughing. He reached for an imaginary shootin' iron on his hip as he clowned, "Would I look fiercer protectin' my propitty if I growed a mustache and pinned thet there tin constable's badge on my manly chest?"

Fierce or not, he had apparently earned the respect of another part of the community.

Vivian Douglas, late 1940s

A Time of Loss

It was a black night one Saturday, in the winter of 1950. With heavy hearts we turned from Highway 7, after finishing our grocery shopping, and crossed the Milwaukee tracks toward home. There, in our driveway, the car lights silhouetted a large fox squirrel carrying a whole ear of field corn in his mouth. He twitched his plumed tail flirtatiously. Stopping the car, we watched him lead a parade of squirrels carrying identical treasures across the driveway from the new corncribs to their hiding places in the grove behind Papa and Mother Douglas's tidy home. They were pilfering from our best corn crop ever, a crop already under the government loan program.

We glanced at the house, and sadness surged to the surface of our minds again. Inside, Don's mother rested with a fragile hold on life. Still courageous and cheerful, she had no hope of recovery. Her trouble had begun less than a year before—when this corn first pushed its green blades through the earth.

As she lost her exuberant energy, Mother Douglas confided her distress too late. She, who had prepared so many meals for all of us, could no longer enjoy them herself. Stomach cancer was diagnosed at the Mayo Clinic in

Rochester, and its ravages were so rapid and pitiless that the doctors advised an operation at once.

She was admitted for immediate surgery and wrote us briefly, "It is cancer, and they may remove part or all of the stomach, or, if they find out it is too advanced, will do nothing." She faced reality honestly and matter-of-factly as she had always done in her roller-coaster life with Papa. From the pleasures of a wealthy farmwife, followed by the ease of retirement at a comfortable lake home, she had been reduced to struggling for a living. Without her enthusiasm and compassion, her life would have been dull drudgery—first on a dairy farm and then on this ranch.

Don took the call from Papa the evening of the operation. It was brief. I read the tragic news in his eyes. As he held me in his arms, he whispered that he had anticipated it and thought his mother had too. But I had never really faced the possibility that this illness might be terminal, and I was overwhelmed. In spite of my work in hospitals, I had no firsthand knowledge of death nor of the kind of suffering that often accompanies it. I ran out of the house, protesting with my body what my mind could not accept.

In those days the word cancer was virtually synonymous with death. I walked until I was exhausted, trying to deal with the insistent questions of why there should be suffering, and why someone so needed, so good, should be taken from us. I kept seeing pictures of Mother Douglas—her slender figure pulling carrots in our big garden, or lifting an angel food cake from the oven, her cheeks pink from the heat. I saw her eyes crinkling with fun as she relayed some amusing neighborhood news, or as she shared bread crusts with the children to scatter for the jaunty squirrels. Until she left for the hospital, she had worked as hard as any of us for that corn crop.

After a few days of worry, Don took care of chores early one morning while I got Anne off to school. Then, with four-year-old Billy, we made the 240-mile trip to Saint Marys Hospital for a hasty visit. She greeted us lovingly as we leaned to kiss her colorless cheeks. When she spied Billy, she strained to raise herself on one elbow to smile and speak reassuringly to him.

When he was only three months old, she had cradled him on her extended arms, his head in the bowl of her hands cupped together. She had crooned to him then, and his gaze fastened on her face. Softly he began to echo back to her the tune of five or six notes. It had been a moment of magic. A bond was established between them that held as long as she lived.

After her return from the hospital she rallied for a while, then we began to observe the waning of her strength from one day to the next. That evening when we dallied in the driveway to watch the squirrels, we'd been bringing home groceries for her household as well as ours. But I no longer had her help, so there was less time than before to spend with her.

Papa, silent and crushed, devoted himself to her. Don and I both yearned to be with her. Don visited his mother nearly every day. When he let the children go along, Anne often carried a dish of tapioca and a labored-over school paper to show. Billy knew that he'd find the bread crusts his grandma never forgot to have ready for him. Together they would stand on her back step for a few moments feeding the squirrels, delightedly recognizing their favorites, and speaking of the ones that were missing the handouts.

Soon the children would come back home, while his mother questioned Don and satisfied her lively interest in every detail of the farm work. She laughed at Don for taking my little 410 shotgun to thin out the rascally squirrels, when he knew they would be quickly replaced from the untold numbers that lived along the river. She watched from her window when a windstorm, common in that flat country, took the roof neatly off of the row of six corncribs—this corn that was now the property of the United States government.

Record crops of corn and wheat in 1948 and 1949 had prompted the Commodity Credit Corporation to set up the Storage Facilities Program. Because local elevators and government storage were overflowing, money was loaned to farmers to build storage on their own land to hold their grain. With the stored corn as collateral, the CCC loaned farmers a "support price." If the market price, in the following July, was greater than the support price, the corn could be sold on the open market, and the farmer would receive the profit. Otherwise, the grain would be turned over to the government. Kurt, the local official of the program, came from his nearby farm to assess the damage. He found the grain remaining in the crib to be in good condition and helped the men get the roof back in place. He advised that we use the corn the wind had swept to the ground for feed.

Hardly a week had passed since Mother Douglas watched the windstorm, when an abrupt call came instructing us to deliver the grain to the elevator in Appleton. Don was puzzled because limited storage was the reason for this program. He always measured generously when he accepted government loan for grain, to be sure its value equaled the money that had been advanced. And so it proved to be. In spite of the squirrels' pilfering, a 25 percent overrun showed up.

"How come," he asked as he signed for his check. "How come mine was the only lot to be called in early?"

"Frankly, we had word you were feeding sealed government-owned grain to your cattle, Don. Sorry, but we'd be liable if we didn't check up, you know. Some fella from down by the river, I think, said he saw you using government grain for your cattle."

"Sweet revenge!" laughed Mother Douglas when he told her of this development. "The 'fella from down by the river' has got to be Olaf. He'll not let you forget you spoiled his deer hunt!"

This corn crop, the last that Mother Douglas would ever see, had been attacked by blackbirds and pheasants, grazed by deer, ogled by frustrated hunters, pirated by squirrels, and exposed by a storm. At last, it was safely out of our hands. She commented that she hoped it would survive its next set of adventures—whether with rats in the elevator or with bureaucrats further down the line.

Her bright spirit masked her declining strength even from our watchful eyes. Suddenly she was gone. I remember her funeral and burial at Benson on a bleak day in February as a blur of misery. My own mourning was delayed, as I tried to be sensitive to Don's and Papa's grief and to soften the sharp edge of loss for the children. Neither of the children really understood, of course, but both were uncommonly subdued throughout the confusion and sorrow of the next few days.

Something deep had been touched in gentle Billy. A few days after the service, he squeezed between me and the sink to "help" me with the dishes. He asked if he could have bread scraps for Grandmother's squirrels.

"Of course. I'm glad you remember and take care of them for her," I answered, clutching his curly blond head to me in a hug so tight it surprised me.

His voice sounded muffled but solemn and determined. "I'm going to be a doctor when I grow up. And I'll make cancer go away."

As always on the farm, the immediacy of the daily tasks demanded our hands and minds and forced a superficial closing of the wound of Mother Douglas's death. I felt drained. From functioning smoothly as a foursome, we now had to find a way to work as three.

I'm sure that farming lost some of its appeal for Don when he lost his mother, whom he resembled so closely in personality. At the same time, though Papa was far from ready to relinquish the reins, he became less ambitious in his planning and allowed Don to take a more vigorous role.

Papa seldom spoke of his Vivian, except to ask for some favorite food she had made. I'll not easily forget, however, his moist eyes and thanks when he picked up the clean laundry I'd mended for him. He kept up his modest home himself and came to us for noon dinner and sometimes supper. His attitude toward me changed subtly. He was more appreciative of little things. He still told his tall tales when he had an audience, but he somehow seemed diminished and vulnerable and so lonely in spite of our best efforts.

The children had gone so often to his home, which

they called the Happy House, when their lively grandmother had been there to welcome them. (I never knew
for sure, but suspected, that the children were told they
must be happy as long as they played at that house.) Now
he enjoyed coming to us as we all tried to assuage the
ache of her absence.

In time, instead of the pain, we learned to remember
the pleasure Mother Douglas had brought us. But for
me, the sight of a field of corn reaching for the sun, or
the saucy flick of a squirrel's tail, continued to bring that
breathless sinking sensation in the chest that is loss.

Marjorie's mother, Olinia, on Papa's horse Ranger

In the Stillness a New Voice

It is sad to remember that Mother Douglas did not live to see our youngest child, Bruce David, who was born the year following her death. How she would have enjoyed him.

This time I did not risk an Island sojourn, but waited at my parents' town home until time for the hospital. A few days after the birth, Dad brought the baby and me back to their home and then drove the older children to the island cottage for days of swimming and learning to handle the canoe and rowboat. Right after Bruce was born, Don had needed to return promptly to the farm. My recovery time alone with my own mother was special for us both.

She pampered me, bringing meals on trays and coffee—which she delighted in serving hot—because she had known mine was often cold before I got around to it at the busy farm table. We enjoyed recollections of her youth and mine, while sharing our delight in the baby.

We talked of the festive Christmases she and Dad had spent with us at the farm. When my parents' car would pull up, the children became excited and irrepressible, until Mother and I despaired of getting at the turkey and

*Anne on the
ski-mounted
box sled, 1944*

our longed-for chance to talk. Dad would unpack the car, with Don's help, and settle the gifts under the tree. After putting the suitcases in the guest bedroom off the kitchen, which doubled as a playroom, he would perform his regular ritual of sharpening my kitchen knives. Dad got his love for beautiful wood and fine tools from his father, a carpenter who lived to be almost 101 in spite of a Civil War wound. Dad taught us as children, and now his grandchildren, how to clean and care for tools. If we ever borrowed a tool, it must be returned in better shape than when we got it. Finally, he would take the children out for a secret journey in the ski-mounted box sled he had made for them, tell them stories, and hunt for the best place to plant day lilies for me the next spring.

At last, Mother and I would be free to prepare the feast for the next day when the Douglases would join us. They would bring their gifts and the crowning glory of the dinner—a steaming plum pudding already melting its golden crown of hard sauce. We ate with sterling silver from the Wedgewood china at a big walnut table in the dining room. A leisurely pace added to the feeling of luxury. We talked of our first farm Christmas when Anne's first sight of the lighted tree so entranced her that she stepped off the staircase into space, missing the last step entirely. The next year my mother gave Anne a toy ironing board, and Anne had to iron twenty doll dresses before she could be persuaded to open another package.

We savored the memories without knowing that the tranquil closeness of these few days together would quickly become another treasured memory. The following winter, Dad and Mother Myers left for an Arizona vacation. My mother, at seventy five, was still able to swim, play tennis, and care for their eight-room house with his help. But when they returned, she had a bout with flu and could not regain her strength. Rapid leukemia was diagnosed, and in only two weeks my mother was gone.

She accepted only one blood transfusion. With its borrowed energy, she arranged for each of my brothers and their wives, who lived at long distances, to come at different times so as not to tax her waning strength. She had chosen to forgo further trips to the hospital for the short-lived benefit of transfusions, saying such a brief and painful survival was not really living. She chose "Now the Day Is Over" for her funeral hymn, at peace with whatever her Maker had in store for her.

The end came on a day when Dad had gone to the sleeping porch utterly exhausted. I stood by her side, gently holding the hand now darkened by hemorrhages, and grieved as her breathing became long trembling gasps and quietly ceased. As the tears flowed, I had the overwhelming feeling that God had stooped near to welcome her spirit. Surely Mother's goodness would not vanish but would survive in some vital, though dimly understood, form.

Dad was desolate, inconsolable as he restlessly visited the homes of his children. Several times he lingered at the farm for a few days, enjoying the children and cradling Bruce in his arms while we revived memories of the island and Mother. My brothers and I and each of our spouses entreated him to make his home with us, but he could not settle down. He considered opportunities for volunteer teaching in poverty settings, even the Peace Corps. Finally he found a new person to "center his life around."

We had always thought of Dad as the strong one in the marriage but now realized Mother had been his balance wheel. He moved into the orbit of his new young wife's family and settled near them in Maryland. Only twice did we manage a visit as this courtly man, who bore the romantic name Walter Raleigh, grew to be a very old man.

Papa Douglas also remarried and moved to a small place that was a part of our farm. He was so near that we occasionally caught a glimpse of him as he took care of his small plantings of corn and soybeans and his few steers, which became like pets. Florence was the longtime widow of Jess Ricke, who had owned the neighboring farm in Benson. The two couples had been friends in Iowa before their moves to Minnesota, and the two Douglas and four Ricke boys had grown up together before becoming stepbrothers. Papa was proud that this vigorous, black-haired lady accepted him, but their children

*Bill Douglas with his
new wife, Florence,
and Rev. and
Mrs. Jackson,
February 14, 1952*

had to cover their surprise. They chuckled to hear of the sparks that flew as the newlyweds adjusted their lives to each other.

While Florence continued to visit her four boys and their families frequently, he preferred his quiet round of duties. He always had an amusing story for the children about a pocket gopher that had burrowed in his front yard when the dog was sleeping, or he'd tell an exaggerated tale of his early days prospecting at a gold mine in British Columbia and see how long he could fool them. He was especially successful with young, trusting Brucie, who always claimed the place on Papa's knee.

With my father in the East and Papa remarried, we felt we had lost all our parents at once. Soon nothing would stand in the way of free choice in our future life—nothing, that is, except a final resolve.

How could we evaluate our growing satisfactions in farming against the rudely disrupted ambitions of nine years before? In the typical hectic summer that followed, visits of old-time friends nudged us toward making that decision.

What a Farm Is Really Like

You're sure the four of you can really sleep crosswise in our seven-foot bed? For one night? You're good sports. We'll love having you."

I slowly replaced the telephone receiver on its hook and then began to laugh. In the aftermath of breakfast for the men, I stood in the kitchen dressed in old jeans and shoes for working in the garden while Bruce took his long morning nap. The phone call was from a sorority sister I had not seen since college days. Now she and her three daughters were following her husband, John Tatam, to a tennis match and wanted to come for an overnight "to see what a farm is really like." For an uncomfortable moment, I was a hybrid again caught between two lives.

"What is a farm really like?" I mused, looking around at the walls once painted a pale sky-blue color—now a bit dimmed. The scuffed linoleum had not been replaced since the redecorating Don and his mother had managed when we moved here nine years before.

My friend was coming to the right place to find out. They planned to arrive the next day for noon dinner. Somehow I found time to stock the refrigerator to the bursting point with fresh fruit and treats and, since the weather was hot, a big container of ice cream. Before I went to bed that night I set the dining room table for ten as the hired men would, of course, eat with us. In the morning I shuffled sleeping arrangements to give the guests our big bedroom, and we and Bruce would use the guest room on the main floor.

The garden was pushing me. I picked tomatoes, which I hoped to peel and stew and can before the arrival of Helen and her girls. Consequently, when the REA shut off power for repairs at eight o'clock, as they did on occasion, I felt utterly helpless. Service was resumed just before eleven o'clock so that I was able to prepare the meal, but three overflowing bushels of tomatoes still crowded the kitchen floor when the guests arrived. Their arms were loaded with gifts of fruit, bakery goods, and even ice cream. The girls were beautifully tanned and healthy looking in their shorts. As they laid their packages on the table, they each thanked me sweetly for letting them come.

The hubbub of the kitchen quieted when the children ran outside with their new friends, although Helen was still hugging me and handing me groceries, which I crowded into the refrigerator. She deluged me with news of the "sisters" she had kept up with. Although I felt adrift from many college friends, I had received some Christmas letters with news, which she welcomed. I glanced at her freshly coiffed hair and comfortable cotton shirt and slacks, set off by a bandanna scarf and a rope belt. Tomorrow she would probably appear in an outfit with a tennis motif. As I struggled with rearranging the food, I was grateful to hear Anne and Bill sharing their pony,

King. The girls took turns trotting around and around the little dooryard, while their mother stepped to the window to watch.

I had barely stowed the perishables when I saw Don and the two hired men arriving promptly for dinner. Why couldn't they be late just this once so I could catch my breath and feel comfortable with my guests? As usual, I did not want to delay the work schedule. Introductions were made as the men leaned over the baskets of tomatoes and washed up at my sink. Then they went to the dining room and stood awkwardly by their chairs in an unaccustomed gesture of courtesy until the little girls finally got their hands washed to their mother's satisfaction, I rejoiced that the pail did not overflow. Unfortunately, while I was busy carrying food to the dining room, my friend, eager to do honor to the occasion, hustled the girls off to change to fresh shorts and shirts while we waited . . . and waited. I knew the men longed to sit down, but I think they sensed that I wanted these guests to get a good impression, and they were determined to be on their best behavior.

Bruce's nap was still "holding" when I finally seated our guests. Helen was gracious and chatty and genuinely interested in everything. I felt as if I could read her mind as she tried one subject after another, not realizing the men would not talk much until they had at least partially satisfied their hunger. As I started the dishes of food around the table and helped the children, I heard Bruce's hungry cry and went to the connecting guest room to tend to him.

I could hear Helen's firm voice. "It's been a great year for tennis," she ventured.

She must have thought that men are always interested in sports. To cover the silence I called a question about John's upcoming match, and Don quickly asked about how he trained and what competition he would face. They chatted briefly.

Apparently determined to involve the hired men, Helen chose middle-aged Bert, who sat at her left. I could imagine his black-whiskered, good-natured face bending over his mashed potatoes and gravy.

"The highway all the way south was beautiful." Pause. "The fields look so pretty. How is the crop here?"

Surely she was thinking that a man always likes to talk about his work. She didn't realize they would feel this was a question only the boss should answer. Don responded courteously but rather briefly for him. Even he found the first business at noon to be food.

Valiantly she tried again, picking up on the children's remarks about the pony. "I suppose you ride horseback a lot, too—in your work—or maybe just to relax?"

This time she was focusing on young, tow-headed Arnold, who lived with his parents in town. He looked up from his nearly empty plate and grinned.

"Yeah, once in a while I get on a horse—if I have to—when the stock gets out or something."

Bert added, "Last night we went after a steer on the tractor." Bert was staying for the summer in the small helphouse and so was available for such duties.

That broke the ice, and the children joined in the laughter. An eager flood of questions began while Don took Bruce on his lap, and Anne helped me serve dessert and more coffee.

Afterwards the young ones, watching where they

stepped in their white tennies, had a memorable visit to the hog barn. Billy had fun being mothered by the youngest guest—a plump, cheerful blonde—as they later ran through the meadow. The girls picked a bouquet of flaming orange field-lilies, pushed Billy in the unusually tall swing that Don had constructed from telephone poles, and then took turns "pumping up" until they could see over the garage. In the late afternoon, we all piled into the farm wagon. Don pulled us behind the tractor to the river while he checked pasture, and Helen and I bumped along enjoying a good chat.

Next morning they claimed they had been able to sleep four in a bed and still emerge fresh and rested. I, too, woke fresh and rested. I had thoroughly enjoyed their visit and realized I had felt no need for apology. For years afterwards, the Christmas cards, from their lovely, river home in Canada, remembered the fun they had had at our farm.

Soon after that, another occasion tested my resourcefulness as a farm hostess. Don's former college roommate, Al Eller, planned to come with his wife, Esther, and his son and twin girls on their way to visit his wife's parents in North Dakota. Our children felt almost as if they knew these friends, for they had more than once listened as we revived memories of school-day adventures.

Anticipating a wonderful catch-up visit, we did not worry about entertaining them, but I had no idea what to feed them. They had become vegetarians! Just then, ready-to-pick peas were a treat, but with only buttered carrots, baked potatoes, a garden salad, and pie, the menu seemed inadequate. Then I found a recipe for a loaf made with nuts instead of meat, and that problem

*Al Eller with Don,
the best man at his
wedding, 1935*

was solved. What I didn't know was that Al, a dentist, had recently forbidden sugar. The family no longer ate sweets of any kind. Feeling that the meal was still a bit slim, I started yeast bread early in the morning and readied two large pans of cinnamon rolls to serve hot with dinner.

The timing was inspired. The big, square, fluffy rolls bubbled with butter and brown sugar as I slid them from the oven. The tantalizing aroma filled the kitchen. Simultaneously, the outside door flew open and our friends burst into the room laughing, hugging, and teasing the children. In the midst of the noisy greetings we soon began to sense that something was amiss. Our kids hung back. They were studying the woebegone expressions of their young guests, who stood glumly regarding the steaming rolls. Al quickly caught on and explained the new "no sweets" rule. Bill and Anne couldn't believe what they were hearing—that children should be forbidden to eat any sweets. My distress must have showed, too. Happily, Al relaxed the rule for the day, and eager smiles returned to the children's faces. I flatter myself that the smell of the fresh baking was almost irresistible to the parents. Instead of pie, I offered fresh fruit and cheese and crackers for dessert, and the dinner could only be called a success. The hot sticky buns vanished with a speed that was amusing.

All too soon, Don and I found ourselves waving and following our friends' car as it started off down the driveway. We felt a vague sense of loss, not knowing when we would see them again. His arm circled my waist, and we began to examine memories stirred by the visit—of our long courtship and our careers in the city.

Restless, we strolled on to the shady railroad ditch where the volunteer asparagus had turned to a feathery foliage. I marked the spot in my memory for next year's harvest. But Don was speaking now, for the first time, of how hard it had been to refuse the job offer as assistant engineer for building the Mexico City airport when we had newly undertaken the work of the farm. He thrived on the management and planning that had fallen more to him these days. Still, he longed for new challenges, and we needed a steadier income. I knew he had resolved to try to sell the farm when the time was right, but he had no idea how difficult it would be to find a buyer. The new owner would have to take over the mortgage on our large farm, with all its machinery and stock, and pay off our growing equity. As we emerged from the shade, the sun glinted on the early silver in Don's hair and burned hotly on the brown of mine. We slowly turned back toward the house, feeling reluctant to plunge at once into ever-waiting tasks.

"One thing you have to say for this life—it keeps us out in the sunshine," I teased. Pointing to Anne, who was leading King back to his stall, I added, "Seriously, it has taught the kids a lot about being responsible and self-reliant."

Don grinned, "Didn't I always tell you how great farming is?"

After a moment, he continued, "It is a good life in many ways. We hadn't exactly figured on eight years, though, had we—and without running water. I distinctly remember telling you two years at the outside. And the end is not yet in sight."

We passed the empty house where for all those years Mother Douglas, like me, had washed her dishes and carried out the slop bucket from under the sink.

"It's different, isn't it," I mused, "since Mother died—I miss her so."

I hoped he would express some of the grief I knew he felt.

He did not answer, and I added, "Does it make a difference in your wanting to stay?"

"Do you hope it does, Marj? You've never complained, and you've worked so hard. This sure as heck isn't the way I planned it for you."

We paused by the burgeoning garden, and I noted tomatoes again ready for canning—perhaps juice this time. He leaned on the fence while I pulled a few weeds. "I honestly don't know, Don. When Helen was here, I listened from the bedroom while I dressed Bruce. Hearing her grope at dinner for some common ground with the men made me realize how much I've changed. I kept hoping she wouldn't ask them how many acres we owned. That seems such a natural question to a city person, but I remember Reub saying it was like asking how much money you have. Now I understand the farmer's attitude, too—about a lot of things. I was right in the middle all through dinner until Arnold loosened things up. He can be such a fun kid."

"About staying," Don persisted, and his earnestness brought my full attention back to what he was saying, "I'm right in the middle, too, in a way. Papa is really pulling back. If he should decide to retire completely, that would leave us free. In the meantime, we're gaining equity, and that's what will be our nest egg for a new business when we leave."

So he wasn't grieving. Like his mother, he accepted the inevitable and was dealing with the reality of the situation—possibilities as well as disappointments.

He pointed in a sweeping gesture from the cornfields in the north to the pastures south of us. "Our equity in this place is still the substitute for the life insurance we sacrificed when we came here, and I'd like to build it up." Eagerness came into his voice. "I bought those feeder cattle to make a good profit. And take a good look at that corn. Perfect. You'll never see better. Maybe we can afford to get a combine and speed up the harvest—jack up the income." His manner changed, and his voice softened. "But it's you I'm thinking of, Marj. You weren't brought up to this, and now you don't have Mother's help. We wouldn't have much to go on, but anytime you say the word, you know that, anytime . . ."

We made our way back to the dooryard, where Bill was twisting up in the swing. Anne had gone back inside with Bruce.

"I'm okay, Don," I interrupted. "The kids are healthy and happy. I wish they had more social life and travel, but until time for college, they'll be fine."

"But you, Marj, you, yourself?"

He sank down on our frequent perch on the steps to the kitchen stoop and coaxed me down beside him.

"We've both invested a lot of ourselves in this life and this community, Don." I answered slowly. "Anne is getting to feel comfortable with her scout group, and her camping experience at Frontenac was positive."

"Yes, and Bill is happy with his Cubs—they liked working on the breadboards we cut out, didn't they?"

"Right. And I've got a few projects of my own going . . ."

"Well, you do seem to like your church study group."

"And my high school discussion class on Sunday: the kids were bringing their friends by the end of the year. I care about those kids, Don. Wouldn't it be hard to pull out right now?"

He considered soberly.

"And you may get a chance to do all the planning around here now, Don. It's no fun to quit until we're ahead. I say, let's give it all we've got—under new management."

Relief and determination were both in his smile. And I knew we would continue, at least for a while, as farmers.

He answered, "So now you're saying farming is great, right?"

Though I still wasn't sure, I did what we often did after serious discussion. I joked. "Well, it took me a little longer than it did Helen, but you have to agree—I finally found out what a farm is really like."

Ripening

Bruce, Bill, and Anne, 1956

Overleaf:
Christmas, 1956. Bruce and Bill had mumps and new red shirts.

The Mad Calf and the Green-Eyed Steer

One dreary, rainy Sunday in the last year of Papa's life he joined us after church for dinner. His second wife Florence was away. When he came to us his vivid stories, of course, came with him. He and Don and the children found it hard to wait as the pot roast bubbled, tantalizing us with its aroma. An hour after it was served, it had vanished completely from the big white platter—along with bright carrots, potatoes, and onions. Only the round marrow bone remained, and even that was scraped clean.

As we finished our strawberries and angel cake, Papa patted his generous stomach and thanked me for a "wonderful dinner that just came out even!" He could not resist a chance to tease, though I could feel him watching my face to be sure I knew it was just that.

He turned his commanding blue eyes toward Don, who sat relaxed at the head of the table, enjoying the peace that comes to a farmer with a full stomach who knows that his animals are also fed and sheltered. Was his contentment really that complete, I wondered. When I had grown restless and felt a need to contribute to some purpose beyond the farm, he backed me. I remembered his support of the two-day training session Donna and I set up for Sunday school teachers, and later he stood behind me as I took on a year's duty selecting and arranging speakers for the PTA. Business, of course, gave him much wider contacts than it gave me. He worked for the Farm Bureau and did occasional township duties, so perhaps he did feel fulfilled. Papa, no doubt, was perfectly content to have Don just where he was.

Papa turned his glance to Anne, who would be twelve that fall. She was disappointed that the rain had spoiled any chance to ride her well-groomed chestnut mare, and so sat there, still wearing her new navy-blue sailor dress. She made restless asides to her mischievous brother Bill, who often spent Sunday afternoon exploring the woods or river with a neighbor boy a year older. Six years younger than Bill, Bruce sat quietly in his high chair beside his grandfather, observing him gravely with large blue eyes so like the old man's. Later people would say that, except for his eyes, Bruce resembled my side of the family with his slender build and olive skin. The older children were big and fair like their father.

When no one made a move to leave the table, Don commented, "For a mad calf roast, that wasn't half bad, now, was it?"

"What do you mean, madcap roast?" Bill demanded quickly, ever alert to his father's voice.

"No, mad calf," Don corrected, smiling secretively.

"You don't mean . . ." Papa looked up in surprise.

"Mean what, Dad? Oh, don't tell. I know! This is the calf someone dumped in our pasture, right? And it attacked you! And no one would own up?" Bill's eyes were wide with excitement as memories came back.

Bruce in his favorite Mexican hat, about 1954

"And you wouldn't let us kids go in there!" Anne remembered, her comments coming all in one breath. "And I caught little Brucie one day sneaking down there—we could hardly even see his Mexican hat as he walked through the hayfield—and he was going to 'bulldog' that calf so it wouldn't hurt Daddy or anyone again. Imagine. The three-year-old hero! He'd have been hamburger for sure."

The color in her face heightened and her vigorous body leaned forward as she gained our attention.

"The very same!" pronounced Don with a laugh.

"Tell, Daddy, please tell—all about it." Bruce loved stories, especially those his father told.

I poured coffee again, and in the enforced leisure of a lazy afternoon indoors, we all settled comfortably in our chairs as Don started his tale.

"It was one of those spring days when you want to find the south side of a warm rock in the sun," he began, "and the grass was coming real good. Scotch thistles and Russian olive seedlings were already spreading all over, so I stopped to cut one out whenever I saw one. Well, I got a big surprise. I counted the feeder calves twice; there was no mistake. I had an extra calf. I had noticed her as I rode up. Sturdy and spotted. Weaned but small—about two hundred pounds. As I got off to look her over—with one foot still in the stirrup—she nailed me so hard I almost went down."

The children looked sober as they tried to picture their strong father threatened by a calf.

"I grabbed her head, threw her down, and then sat on her." That drew a giggle from Anne. "She seemed to be in good condition. Then I jumped up quickly and made it into the saddle before she could get up to charge me again. Believe me, she was willing! I couldn't figure out what made her so mean—never did, as a matter of fact.

"Seven other farm pastures come up against ours, but not one of those men admitted to owning that calf. Next week the calf was still there and as bad tempered as before. I kept trying to peddle that calf but got no takers.

"I didn't want any of you kids to get near the pasture. Bruce, you promised to wait to tackle a steer until you're grown up, remember?"

The child nodded solemnly. Don's voice deepened as he continued, and I heard in it his concern over Bruce's lack of caution in his desire to be a helper like Anne and Bill.

"So, I decided to drive the cattle up to the feed yards and sort her off. We put her in an eight-by-eight-foot stall by herself. We had to feed and water her, naturally, and clean the pen. Every time we came near her, she'd put her head down, tail up, and make a run at us. Sometimes I ended up with a bent bucket, but that's about all. Whenever I got to town or farm meetings, I inquired for the owner but had no takers. And she never gentled down.

"By early winter—with all the extra feed—she was nearly eight hundred pounds, I'd say, and I needed the room she was occupying in the barn. Lawyer Kivley had a good laugh at my expense when I asked him what to do with her. He bunched up his bushy eyebrows and scowled at me, and said, 'You can't sell her. You would be breaking the law if you sold something that wasn't yours. The only thing I can think of is to eat her.' Accordingly, I put a lariat around her neck and allowed her to chase me into the pickup box, while Papa tied her down to a ring in the floor. We fastened a partition over the top of the box."

Honesty, fairness, safety precautions—I hoped the children were absorbing it all along with the story.

"She was always ornery," he continued, "but that heifer was downright menacing by the time we reached the local locker plant. Before I gave the end of the rope to that husky butcher, I explained to him the unfriendly nature of the critter.

"He answered, 'Yeah, yeah, yeah! I handle this stuff all the time.'

"I insisted, 'She's a maverick. She's really mean. She doesn't give you time to think.'

"He answered shortly, 'Give me the rope and get out of the way.'

"So I did."

The children gasped, and I heard another nervous giggle from Anne, but they did not interrupt.

"I opened the endgate of the truck and instantly the half-grown animal went on the attack. She sure was ready for him. She had bottled up her rage all the way to town. She chased that butcher onto the killing floor and kept him dodging faster than I thought a man of his build could move. He finally got the rope around the sturdy center post and just stood there puffing and wiping the sweat off his forehead.

"When he got his breath back, he had the grace to grumble, 'You're right about that one!'"

The children laughed delightedly. Don had a self-satisfied look as he said, "Now aren't you surprised the mad calf's meat tasted so good and was so tender?"

"Your mother had the right touch with it, didn't she?" Papa put in. I detected a peace offering in that remark in case my feelings had been hurt earlier. I smiled at this man whose life had been so greatly altered. His bulk, like the butcher's, was considerable, and he had enjoyed the description of the other man's lively dance around the center pole on the killing floor. With his gift for apt names he immediately dubbed the story, "The Mad Calf and the Maypole," and so it was.

While the grownups reminisced, the boys began whispering animatedly, then Bruce slipped away from the table and soon came running back waving his red jacket. At the signal, Bill immediately began a singsong chant of "Toro, toro, toro" and was ready to act out a bullfight right there.

They quickly settled down again when Papa asked, "Did you children ever see a steer's eyes turn green? No? Well, if you ever do, it's a signal to get out of the way and quickly. Like I saw your daddy do once."

"Why, Papa?"

"What happened?"

He held out his coffee cup, cream and sugar were passed, and he stirred and stirred while the children fidgeted. Papa enjoyed having everyone's attention, and he knew how to stretch out the suspense and then tease them along.

"Well," he began at last, "one evening your daddy and I were over by the Cairns farm, driving the cattle home from summer pasture. They were especially spooky and hard to handle. It took longer than we figured to separate ours from Cairns' stock, and by the time we got them started down the road, dark was settin' in. When we got them crowded together, they filled the roadway, so we borrowed a lantern from our friends, and just in time 'cause I saw a car comin' mighty fast. I ran out into the middle of the road and swung it back and forth, but this dern fool driver kept a-comin' like sixty!

"It was dry last year, you know, or we'd never have had to rent pasture. But you don't remember that, do you? Last year you were all just little duffers, weren't you, too little to remember—"

"Oh, Papa," Bill protested. Himself prone to tease, he was now impatient with delay and eager for the story. "Did the driver hit you? Did the dern driver get stopped in time?"

But Papa was still paying out line and not at all ready to satisfy their curiosity.

"No, I jumped out of the way. He didn't hit me, but just picture it, Billy. That road is narrow and graveled, and the side ditches are shallow 'cause the ground is flat. Here we were with thirty head of feeders that were used to running with the others in the pasture and hadn't learned to stay bunched. Your dad was about worn out with chasing to keep the stragglers together. We would have been home before dark if they'd behaved."

"But Papa—the driver?"

"The driver, dern his skin, speeded up—told us afterwards he thought we were trying to hold him up. How about that? Well, he had a banged-up radiator to show for his foolishness. Hold him up, huh!—with thirty heifers and steers milling around!"

"But what happened, Papa, what happened?" This time it was Anne who impatiently took the bait. "What did he hit?"

"He hit the steers, that's what happened. You can't imagine what a bloody mess. And the racket! Don and I both yelled a warning, but the driver was so busy leaning on his horn he couldn't hear. That alone would have been enough to stampede the steers, and, of course, they scattered in every direction. One died on the spot—its neck was broken. The car careened off the road. We didn't realize till later that it had hit another steer and smashed its leg. That one we had to butcher. By the time the wreck was over, the car itself was at a crazy angle. It had ended up in the ditch with a wheel on top of a third steer.

"The tall, skinny driver managed to climb out and came toward us waving his arms and hollering, 'You wrecked my car! Your blasted cows wrecked my car!'

"I hollered right back, 'You get your blasted car off my cow!'

"Well, the three of us managed to cool down enough to lift it off, and that steer was right glad to get up and hightail it off to the boondocks. The tall Norwegian must have figured out that was the best idea for him, too, 'cause he revved up out of the ditch and took off down the road with his radiator leaking and one wheel bumping the fender. That was the last we ever saw of him.

"It was full dark before we were able to drive the steers into our pasture. Except for the dead ones and three that had gone wild."

He paused, a thoughtful look on his face. Bruce, of course, began to mourn over the hurt animals, but Bill thought, as a good farmer does, and asked, "What happened to those three? Did they run away? Did you ever get them home?"

Anne had been thinking, too, and dared to call her grandfather to task. "What about the green eyes, Papa? You warned us about green eyes."

His thoughtful look dissolved into one of sly pleasure over keeping his audience still firmly hooked, and he warmed to his story again.

Apparently ignoring Anne, he continued, "We let them go till morning, Bill. 'There's a time for every purpose under Heaven,'" he said, intoning his favorite verse from Ecclesiastes. "'A time to get and a time to lose.' Well, we lost those two which were killed, but we dern well meant to get the last three. After breakfast we took a tractor and a box wagon. We found the steers at the south end of Cairns' pasture. Two steers went up the ramp and into the wagon very easily, but the third was a problem. He was the one the car had sat on. Big and brown with white spots over one eye, he balked every time we got him to the ramp. I expect he remembered that car coming at him and all the noise and shoutin'. Your dad got a halter on him, slick as any cowboy, and he pulled and pulled, but that critter must have weighed seven hundred pounds. Wouldn't you say, Son?"

Don nodded, amused at his father's enjoyment in manipulating the children. Over many years, Don had learned his own quiet method of coping with his father's ways.

"About the third time we got him to the foot of the ramp, Don pulled and I pushed and shouted. The steer put his head down and snorted, then threw his head back, hoisted his tail up like a battle flag, and his eyes turned as green as a frog in spring. Your dad was standing in the wagon box, but when this crazed animal charged up the ramp and in, your dad just wasn't there. He vaulted over the front of the wagon and ducked, just in time to see the steer sail clean over the front of the wagon and over his head to the ground beside the tractor. It's a wonder the animal didn't break a leg, but no, all we could see was the north end of him going south and fast.

"We decided right then and there to give Old Green Eyes a couple more cooling-off days. When we did go back a second time, he was quiet as a lamb. You'd think he'd never had an ugly thought in his head."

"I'm glad Dad got out of there in time, like you said, Papa." Billy was solemn—whether in awe of his father's speedy reflexes or whether he was already imagining a game of jumping over the endgate of the wagon—it was impossible to tell.

I, too, was glad Don had got out of the way in time. Farmers we knew had fingers or hands missing; one had lost an arm and now used a hook. At that moment, the thought came to me that Papa's spirit of fun was an important survival tool. This business of farming was full of unexpected peril.

Time kept slipping by since we had moved here to help out. Eleven years ago we had bought in as partners and now were wondering when Papa would want to retire. Don still had his health, although on three terrifying occasions the unrelenting work had literally brought him crawling back to the house. Did we want to finish out our days on the farm?

Suddenly Anne broke into my thoughts by exclaiming, "We'll call it the story of 'Green Eyes and the Disappearing Cowboy.'"

It was not the first time she had stolen her grandfather's thunder. Was that a little flash of jealousy on his face? It was fun to see someone tease Papa, and I think he liked it, too. When I looked again, I could see only pride in his expression. Perhaps he was thinking that, long after he was gone, his granddaughter and the boys, too, would enliven many good beef dinners with a retelling of his favorite stories.

The Whist Club at Battle Lake, late 1950s. Back row: Don, Lester Kerr, Miles Cunningham, Alvene Cairns, Abigail Evans, Willem Curry, Mark Cunningham, Taylor, Willie Evans; front row: Howard Cairns, Marjorie, Patty Cunningham, Alma Timm, Nora Cunningham, Grace Curry. Abigail and Willie were frequent substitutes; Gus and Alvina Hartkopf are missing; Kurt Timm must have taken the photo.

We Join the Whist Club
and Willem Tells a
Story, He Does

One Saturday night in 1954, about eight o'clock, the children had just gone to bed and Patsy Cairns was placed in charge. Don and I eagerly awaited the couple from the farm a mile west of us. When they pulled up to the gate, I could see Grace Curry's smiling face in the ghostly glare of our yard light as she reached to swing the rear car door open for me. I was startled to notice how much smaller Willem looked sitting under the steering wheel than sitting on the tractor in the field. There he gave the impression of being a tremendous man with bulging shoulders. But there was nothing small about Willem's voice, trained in auctioneering, which began greeting us exuberantly as we came across the dooryard and now filled the sedan.

Don had worked at threshing with Willem and described him as *attacking* work, instead of just shoveling grain or loading bundles as the others did. He claimed there was just no wear-out to Willem. This short, stocky farmer had been in my kitchen on several occasions, and the energy of voice and body made the kitchen seem confining. His speech was loud, repetitious, and emphatic, but usually good natured and mixed with hearty laughter. Before the car doors were shut, he launched into a story to entertain us as we drove two miles north to our first evening with the Whist Club, which our neighbors Howard and Alvene Cairns had invited us to join.

Until we came into the Whist Club, Alvene had been the youngest; yet she mothered us all and we grew to depend on her love and wisdom. As town librarian three afternoons a week, she felt obliged to read every new book and could recommend one of particular interest for every patron. Any books she found unsuitable for young readers she kept out of sight under her desk and circulated them only on request. Her husband's quiet, dignified bearing covered a devilish streak he apparently had—judging from the stories of his youth.

One day Howard was chatting about having joined the parade of young fellows driving their cars down Appleton's Main Street every Saturday night.

Don looked at him quizzically for a moment, then hazarded a guess. "And you were an expert at making your Ford Model A backfire to get the girls' attention."

Howard bugged his eyes at him in surprise. "You weren't living around here then. How did you know I had a Model A Ford?"

Don laughed, delighted he had hit the mark. "Well, I had one and I know you, and I know you'd have had one—and would have known how to make it perform."

There was a meeting of minds between them in many ways, and the four of us and our families became very close.

On that first night at the Cairnses, we had to wait for the ninth couple. We sat with Willem and Grace, who made sure we knew everyone. Except for Don and me,

Main Street, Appleton, looking south, mid-1930s—with a Model A at left and the Methodist Church steeple in the distance, at left

only one other couple were not neighbors. They also were not farmers. Taylor, a sportsman and a school superintendent in a small town nearby, contributed his cynical, amused outlook on life. His wife, Florence, a lively school librarian, roused the envy and admiration of all the women with her flair for art and home decoration. Miles, a farmer and rural mailman east of town, had remarried after the death of his first wife. We all enjoyed Patty, his present wife, with her convivial ways and lavish hand with rich food. Gus and Alvina, Alma and Kurt, and Lester and Fern rounded out the group; when Mark and Nora arrived, we could start.

Although Don and I had lived near Appleton for eleven years, we were still, in a sense, outsiders to this group of our neighbors. Most of them had gone to grade school and high school together. We also had never played whist. My feeling a stranger to the group was heightened by all my impressions that first evening with these new friends. At the last of the four tables I played partner to tall, laconic Gus who, I later learned, found time to play cards uptown after morning chores nearly every day. Not surprisingly, Gus was a highly skilled and intuitive card player, so his score was often the winning one. We played four hands at each of four tables. I did not realize that the score at each table was added to the preceding one, so I kept adding my totals, instead of my game scores, giving me a phenomenal score, which gave Gus ammunition with which to tease me ever after.

"Is this the real score or your padded score?" he would ask.

Don meanwhile played partner to Alma, a clever, strong-minded, and outspoken woman. When the game was explained to Don, he was told to show a red card if he wanted to play his hand to lose tricks and a black one if he wanted to take tricks. Everyone around the table thus "bid" for how the round should be played. Oddly enough, on that first hand he had been dealt thirteen red cards so had no choice but to show a red card. The hand was played "low," that is, to take as few tricks as possible. But Don couldn't manage to lose the lead. He took every trick. Alma was furious. She scolded him loudly and thoroughly before he could reveal that he held no black cards. She promptly began all over again to castigate him for not explaining his problem at the beginning.

Hardly a propitious beginning for a friendship, but Don and Alma seemed to understand each other. "You have to learn how to take Alma," Don used to say when I got worked up over an argument with her.

He liked to tell about the day he stopped at their home on business and found family and hired man just sitting down to dinner. His greeting from Alma was, "I suppose you came right at dinner time thinking I'd have to invite you to stay. How did you know we were having chicken and homemade ice cream?"

Don appraised the situation, then pulled up a chair saying, "You're damn right I did! That's the chance you take being such a great cook!"

Don had an appetite to match his size and loved to eat. But that day he knew he was eating an outstanding meal, and I'm sure he did it full justice. She loved him for it.

Don knew all the men and many of the women, but I had had little opportunity to meet people. I did know Alma, her brother, Lester, and his wife Fern, because they also attended the Methodist church. As nearly as we could figure out, this brother and sister loved pretending to be enemies and made no secret of their squabbles. Lester and Fern enjoyed entertaining the group so much that they built a fireside room, with space for the four tables and a buffet, onto their already large and comfortable home. With Alma and her husband Kurt, they inherited a cottage at Battle Lake, where once a year the Whist Club had a house party. The women slept in the house, the men in a converted chicken house. We swam and picked wild strawberries for a shortcake feast and played cards.

At Battle Lake, Grace and Alma always made sure there was plenty of fishing. One year a gusty wind prevented our using the pontoon boat till afternoon, when eight of us crowded onto the flat deck. Don started the little trolling motor and guided us to the favorite fishing spot near some reeds. Five friends soon vied for space at the railing to fish. Inevitably their lines tangled. All managed to extricate themselves except Lester, with his expensive rod and lure, and his sister Alma, with her well-used pole and battered Bass-oreno lure. They yanked and yanked to free their lines but only tangled them further. Ever impatient, Alma exploded when she heard Grace exulting over pulling in a nice smallmouth bass. Giving Lester's line one more yank, she said sharply, "Here, I'll cut your line, Lester, and we'll start over."

"Not mine, you won't," Lester retorted. "That's a brand new fifteen-pound test line and a new No-Fail lure. Yours is the old one. Cut yours!"

While they did battle, Don pulled in both lines, removed the baits and hooks, and patiently sorted out the mess now laced with slimy weeds. When the combatants got busy reattaching their hooks, he again started the engine—only to find we had drifted to an exposed position where the wind was driving our overloaded boat straight to the opposite shore. The accolades heaped on Don, the peacemaker, only a moment before quickly turned to mock criticism for Don, the pilot. For me, this group was an ever-unfolding experience of friendly, nonjudgmental human beings who accepted each other as they were. The noisy joking may have masked the anxiety about water that is common to farm people. We let ourselves be blown ignominiously to the wrong shore, where we tied up to a tree. Then we trudged single file around the end of the lake and back to the cabin to endure the taunts and ribbing of the rest of our friends.

But it was on that first night that I got a special insight into their friendships. The ninth couple at last showed up. Miles's handsome brother, Mark, was casual and joking as usual. His wife Nora, however, looked flushed and her thick yellow hair was ever so slightly untidy. She had dressed for the party while Mark finished milking. In hurrying to clear up, she managed to spill a full pint of heavy cream into her drawer of cutlery. A meticulous housekeeper, she did not even consider leaving the sticky mess.

At last we drew tally cards and settled down at the assigned tables. During the evening I was often aware of Willem's powerful, slightly grating voice. Once his stately wife, Grace, played at my table. Again I admired the thick, curly white hair framing her regular features. I knew she was able to operate any of the machinery on their tidy farm and worked side by side with Willem at the milking and feeding chores. One of the many things Grace later taught me was how to improve my bread making by kneading the dough until it glistened.

At the end of the evening when my tally was revised, it showed a medium score, but Don had one of the two lowest and had to wash dishes. The "lunch," which was served after midnight because of our late start, proved to be a hearty dinner. Afterwards we settled down for a couple of hours of visiting and gossiping. Then I began thinking of Sunday school duties the next morning and wondered if we dared suggest leaving. In a moment I became aware of an expectant hush. Red-headed Mark had happened to speak of a former neighbor who had died several years before. The mention of her name triggered a story of Willem's that was apparently one of his favorites. His voice rose, drowning out the others. Grace stirred uneasily in her chair. Eyebrows were raised in otherwise impassive faces. I made a guess that the story was painfully familiar to all the others.

"So I told them, 'Sure, I'd be a pallbearer, I would,'" he was saying.

A good choice, I thought—in those days of heavy coffins. Willem had the strength and stamina to be a good pallbearer. He bragged that he could work early and late in the field, then bull through two hours of chores and still dance all night—as long as a good German band was playing. For a stunt, he waltzed balancing a glass of wine on his shoulder. He insisted that he never spilled a drop.

"And the funeral was set for 10 A.M. on August eleven, it was," the noisy torrent of Willem's voice continued. "That was back in nineteen hundred and . . ."

But Gus broke in—rudely, I thought. "Willem, it couldn't have been 10 A.M. Father John was at Holy Rosary Church then, don't you remember? You know he never had a funeral in his life as late as ten o'clock. You had to get up at the crack of dawn to get milking done if you wanted to make it to church."

The point was hotly argued at some length. Gus finally conceded the point, and Willem plunged in again.

"The ushers put the pallbearers into the second pew from the front, they did, right behind the family. I went in first so I was way over at the side by the big pillar. The church was crowded, it was, and hot. The sun come right in our faces—"

"Why, Willem," Gus was at it again, his voice chiding. "The sun couldn't have been coming in those front windows, not in the morning, not in the fall." I was really squirming by this time, wondering why he didn't let the poor man tell his tale. But we were forced to listen as a lively discussion raged about the curve of the driveway and its angle to the highway and the exact placement of the church. This time Mark and then Miles joined in baiting the storyteller, supporting Gus, who was usually a man of few words. Alvene gave Nora a secretive smile, and I saw Patty glance curiously at Grace. Now I was sure that my guess had been correct. No one wanted to spoil good-hearted Willem's story, but they felt entitled to amuse themselves a bit at his expense.

Willem's voice commanded attention as he continued filling in every detail. "Well, this Alice, she was from away somewhere—a cousin, I think, of the deceased—she sat directly in front of me, she did. Then we all stood, out of respect, you know, and suddenly it was just too much for this poor lady. She keeled right over, she did, down onto her knees on the floor—kerplunk! I just reached over the back of the pew, I did, and grabbed her under the arms, I did, and hauled her up to her feet. She wasn't tall, but she was heavy! Well, she didn't seem to be able to stand—went right down again limp-like, she was." Willem was getting pretty excited, and the words just spouted out of him.

"I lifted her up again, I did. Poor thing. She was crying now." I heard suppressed laughter, but Willem was oblivious. "And I was really sweating, I was, but as soon as I let go, darned if she didn't go down again."

His voice dropped a little. "Then I noticed all the family, the relatives and all, was on their knees just like her. Yup, they was Catholics, they was, most every one."

The laughter surged, explosive at first, then—we were all tired and the evening had been long—we continued laughing helplessly. We laughed at Willem. We laughed with Willem. We laughed because the others laughed. It became a spiral of laughter. The men slapped their legs and guffawed, the women dabbed at their eyes and held their stomachs. I had hidden my amusement at the double comedy—first out of "politeness," then from embarrassment. When I finally let go, I laughed till my throat ached. Still, underneath it all, I wondered about Willem and Grace. Had this teasing, which seemed unkind to me, hurt their feelings? They appeared to be entirely at ease. These people were practical, honest, outspoken farmers. Sometimes they were earthy in their talk and rough in their humor, but they were loyal to a fault and totally accepting of each other. They were closer, really, than many families.

Butch

Heaven knows there was plenty for me to do on that big western Minnesota farm without chickens to care for. But I've always been sinfully fond of eating chicken —whether fried, baked, or cut up in a salad— it doesn't matter. I love chicken. In all my previous city life I had seldom fully satisfied my craving. Perhaps an unconscious wish to have all the chicken I could possibly want made me listen so willingly to the siren talk of my Whist Club friends about farmwives' "egg money" and all the things it bought. Because times were still hard in the mid-1950s, I frequently asked my husband why we didn't keep chickens if they paid so well. He scoffed, saying the women took the gross income and called it profit. They didn't figure in, he pointed out, the shelter, feed, or labor for which their husbands paid. My eleven years on the farm did not make me an expert, and I meekly accepted his wisdom.

Then we'd return to the Whist Club and I'd hear again of the easy profits of the chicken business. In the back of my mind I clung to the thought that such hard-working, realistic, honest farm women knew what they were doing when they chose to raise chickens. As I persisted, my husband finally decided to indulge my whim (more like a fixation by this time). He not only indulged me—he did it in a big way. He suggested we try the chicken business as a serious sideline. We both let ourselves hope that a chicken business on a large scale would become a significant source of additional income. He fitted out one of the one-hundred-foot barns with nests and roosts where 1,100 hens were soon confined. The children and I learned to help pick and wash eggs and sort them into cartons holding twelve dozen apiece.

Although the men tended the waterers before and after fieldwork, it came as something of a surprise to me that water had to be added to the troughs during the day. Carrying water was not my favorite occupation, and I already had more of that duty than I wanted. I had no way to store more than the two two-and-a-half-gallon pails that stood on my sink drainboard. A similar pail stood in the cabinet under the sink to catch the waste water. I kept it on a blanket of newspaper in case I forgot to empty it before it overflowed. In bad weather one of the men usually got the water for me, especially on washday, but the two buckets seldom lasted a half day. Special tasks—such as washing garden produce and canning, or bathing the children—required many extra trips. Now, I had succeeded in adding 1,100 thirsty hens to my chores.

Carrying the water was a constant aggravation. In our early days at the farm, Don had hired a professional driller to deepen the well and pipe water to and from the house. At 165 feet, the limit for the equipment, the sand-point was making progress only a fraction of an inch at a time through a thick layer of blue clay. The heavy electric motor brought up barely sufficient water, and the project

Anne, 12, and Marjorie

had to be abandoned. Water carrying was a fact of life. Now Bruce, at two, was my "helper" and eagerly filled his toy buckets and hurried along at my side.

We had to pick eggs twice a day. Anne, with her long slender hands, excelled at this. Mischievous Bill found it hard not to excite the birds, but his incredibly quick reflexes helped him sneak the eggs out from under a hen's fluffed-up feathers before she had time to react. Except for one hen. Oh, how we all hated that hen. She was always broody, and we suspected that she changed nests to hatch eggs that other hens had laid. She always covered several eggs and was fiercely protective of them. Let a hand slip under her ever so slowly, and, just as it grasped the fragile egg, her sharp beak bit the tender skin on the back of the wrist.

Other hens pecked us and let go, but this old dragon lady held the pinch of skin in her beak and twisted, leaving a bloody bruise. Often the children complained to their father, who was unimpressed. Finally they talked him into going himself to pick the eggs from under this one hen. They found her full of self-importance, firmly ensconced on a nest. Anne and Bill stood at a little distance as their father quietly approached and gently slipped his hand under her exactly as he had taught them. It looked as if he might succeed. They watched tensely. In a flash she had a pinch of his flesh, but as she twisted, Don grabbed her by the neck and threw her hard against the floor. The next day we had her on our dinner plates, and Don wore a bandage on the back of his wrist. Anne and Bill never let him forget that they deserved to be listened to.

Many eggs got cracked even after we became more skillful in taking care of them. I no longer felt extravagant in making twelve-egg angel food cakes and sponge cakes the next day to use up the yolks—as well as omelettes and souffles. Don bought nothing but the best supplemental feed for flavor and crushed oyster shell to make the eggshells firm. He even had some of the hens fitted with metal "glasses" when they turned cannibalistic. This interfered with their line of vision in a way that prevented their pecking each other. Nothing I observed about the chickens made them seem the slightest bit lovable or responsive, and long before the end of a year the whole enterprise became burdensome. Don had kept careful cost accounting, and when a study of our records showed that our year's work had put us six hundred dollars in the red, he quickly arranged for a sale of the chickens. Coupons had been given when he bought feed and supplies or sold eggs. Now we gathered up the year's accumulation of coupons and redeemed them for what is still known as the Six Hundred Dollar Card Table.

"Use this," my husband said the day the truck was coming to take the chickens to the market. He handed me a sort of shepherd's crook he had fashioned out of heavy wire. "As they load, if you see a nice fat hen, snag it by the legs, and throw it over that low door into the feed room. We'll fill our locker and have at least something to show for our year's work."

I kept thinking of the new recipes I had collected from the Whist Club. I could almost taste the delicious chicken. Don, not as enthusiastic about eating chicken as I, still had said to take all I wanted. The shepherd's crook required little skill. A quick flick caught the legs of my chosen bird. A hen, too surprised to cackle, was swung limply over the low door and disengaged in mid-flight. I soon developed a rhythm. I really caught on to using that crook.

But eighty-five birds? I couldn't believe the flapping, clucking crowd of birds I met when I opened the feed room after the truck pulled out. I shut the door quickly and leaned weakly against it.

Never in my city-bred life had I killed a chicken or anything else—unless you count angleworms for fishing. As it happened, my husband and the hired man were busy doing custom hay-baling along with their regular fieldwork. All the help they offered was lots of advice.

The next morning, as soon as they left the house, I set about my new challenge. It sounded as if the least bloody method was to grasp the bird by the head and swing her high and violently in a great circle, thereby breaking her neck. I'd never seen it done, but it sounded promising. I gave it my best, not once, but twice. It didn't work the second time either, although the children at the kitchen window looked impressed by the maneuver. More than a little abashed, I moved, with what I hoped was a show of confidence, to method number two. Placing a foot on the now befuddled creature's head, I yanked—energetically.

There's a good deal to be said for technique. All I can say is that I didn't have any. Fortunately the poor hen was feeling a bit peaked by this time and squatted with her feathers ruffled and her head pulled in, while I rushed for the axe—method number three. I firmly believe no one had ever sharpened that axe, and determination was no substitute for a sharp edge. When I chopped and chopped again, amazingly hitting my now gun-shy target in roughly the region of the neck, the axe bounced. Worse, the hen made a pathetic, pleading sound much like the croak of a bullfrog in mating season.

I was undone. Nervous tears started. When I glanced up at the window, the watching children looked blurred. They stared wide-eyed, and their heads were wreathed with what appeared to be steam. Startled out of my self-pity, I ran to turn off the kettles of water boiling to defeather my intended morning run of birds.

When I thought I had my feelings under sufficient control, I phoned Papa's wife.

"Florence," I asked, sounding as light and casual as I could manage, "how do you kill a chicken?"

I had failed miserably even at controlling my voice, for the reply came firmly, "Hold everything, Marj. I'll be right over."

She proceeded to hang the poor creatures by their heads from the wire clothesline. Their weight pulled the neck vertebrae apart, and one capable stroke of the butcher knife freed the bodies for a final, sickening caper, headless, around the yard. The kids liked this best of all. We did not finish all eighty-five birds that day, but the pace picked up remarkably.

And me? Well, my appetite eventually returned. As I said, I really love chicken. But, for many years, when my husband wanted to puncture my ill-advised enthusiasm for some new project, he had only to use the nickname "Butch" to revive the memories of his overambitious management and my butchering of the hens.

Don and understudy Bill, about 1956

A Bitter Experience

The tractor came thundering up the lane, throttle wide open. Rage flooded through me, unfamiliar and unbidden.

The men had returned to the field after noon dinner, and the dishes had been hastily washed and put away "Quiet time" had finally arrived—with Anne deep in a book and Bruce in his bedroom napping with his teddy bear or "reading" his picture books. All week I had labored to gain time to finish a woolen shirt I had started to sew for Don's birthday. The overabundance of strawberries and rhubarb from the garden was canned. I had earned some time for myself. I could almost taste the fun I would have tailoring the gray-and-blue-striped woolen material I had so optimistically chosen.

Just under the surface of my mind, of course, was the unsettling concern about Bill, who liked to think of himself as a farmer and who constantly teased for permission to go to the field with the men. Neither Don nor I believed children belonged near machinery, and certainly not at age ten. But when the men had decided that our bluegrass in the south pasture was heavy enough to strip for seed, Don promised the boy he could have the job of holding the sack when the driver emptied the stripper at the end of each row. As it happened, after the arrangements were all made, the man who usually drove the tractor disappointed us. A high-school neighbor boy filled in. We were not very comfortable with the arrangement but hated to disappoint Billy.

Papa liked to say, "One boy is fine. Two boys make half a boy. Three boys mean no help at all." Although we did not feel comfortable with the decision, we finally agreed to let the boys go ahead as planned. We made them agree that Bill would not help with the tractor nor the stripping machines. He could not ride the tractor, nor would the tractor be driven faster than second speed. Bill was so earnest. He waited for our answer in so poised and tense a manner, his whole attitude reflecting the eagerness that shone in his eyes. We knew that we had to let him help. When he finally had our permission, he donned his sister's outgrown cowboy boots and strutted—just a little— as he imagined himself to be the handy, capable farmer he longed to be.

Now I couldn't believe what I heard. In spite of the most solemn promises, here came the tractor without the strippers. It was racketing up the lane, raising a cloud of dust. Only an hour ago I had watched them carefully pussyfoot away, Bill walking dutifully alongside. He was now breaking another rule by riding on the draw bar. As I ran to the dooryard gate, my fury, fed by beginning apprehension, started to overflow in angry words before I saw his right arm held above his head. As they braked to a stop, I realized that bright blood was dripping from it. My voice squeaked to a halt, my mouth suddenly dry and throat aching, as if I had been running for a long time. Was his hand cut or torn? Was his hand repairable? Heart pounding and arms outstretched, I ran to him. Then I could see that the last phalange of the right index finger had been severed. Should we be hunting for the missing part on the unlikely chance that it could be surgically reunited? As I saw the tags of skin hanging empty, I knew there was no hope of that. He had stumbled as he walked beside the stripper and reached out his hand for balance; the tip of his finger was caught and ground through a gear. He did not cry or complain. His finger must still have been numb from shock. I saw him to the car, then dashed to the kitchen for clean tea towels to catch the drips of blood and support the hand. At the same time I yelled for Anne, who obediently gathered up Bruce and took him into the back seat with her.

We dashed to the hospital and fortunately found the doctor in. He anesthetized the hand, gave Billy a tranquilizer, and began to fashion a neat new tip on the second joint of the truncated finger.

A nurse shepherded Anne and Bruce to a waiting room where Anne was soon entertaining her brother and two other young boys with her usual aplomb. I managed to stand beside Bill, who was remarkably calm, with only the touch of my hand to reassure him. What I remember now is their cleaning away the poor scraps of skin and folding the best of what was left over the stump. The finality of what had happened weighed more and more heavily on me. The end of the finger was gone and could not be brought back. I suffered excruciating pangs of guilt. We should not have let the child persuade us against all our principles—no matter how great his disappointment.

That is what I remember before my legs began to tremble and my skin to prickle and sweat. Knowing the signs of faintness and not wanting to interrupt the work, I stepped into the hall where I had seen a davenport. I stretched out there, deeply shaken by the finality of Billy's injury. Dizziness spun the room around. It was not the first time one of us had been injured, but this time nothing could be done. As I closed my eyes and gripped the edge of the davenport to steady myself, I saw a clear image of Don, his face distorted in pain, crawling back to the house on hands and knees after his back "went out" when he was pitching feed to the livestock. Our doctor, a small man who could not overcome the involuntary protective contractions of that strong back, sent him to the chiropractor, who prevailed. In my mind, Bill's bleeding finger again appeared, as it would so many times in the following years—an empty shell with no nail, no flesh, no bone, only mangled skin tags hanging loose and empty. Faintness swept over me, and I gripped the cushions with all my strength.

My vision was clearer now, and again I saw Bill as he looked early this afternoon—a little boy innocent of danger, reaching and straining to become a man like the father he adored. Were we doing right by keeping him on the farm? Were we limiting his choices?

The moments of anger, apprehension, fright, and useless denial were behind me. As I regained my strength and prepared to take the children home, grim reality set in. I could have taken a lesson from the victim, who wasted no energy on regrets. Much more than I, he truly had the temperament to be the farmer he wanted so much to be. He cheerfully reminded me that he was lucky to be left-handed, since it was the right one that was injured.

A New Bond

I suppose I should have known that horses are an integral part of life on a stock farm. But it took me a while. My early childhood memory of horses was of the jaded ponies parading endlessly around the top floor of Dayton's department store or at Longfellow Gardens near Minnehaha Park.

I was hardly prepared when, early in our acquaintance, Don began to talk of horses as friends with personalities. He told of the pet pony he saddled when he was a little boy not yet strong enough to pull the cinch tight. He and the saddle slid until they hung under the pony's belly. The pony waited patiently for Don to disentangle himself before taking another step.

He told of inadvertently sharing a box stall with a terrified stallion during a violent thunderstorm. Though the animal pitched and bucked and kicked, he somehow spared Don. He spoke fondly of a pair of fiery matched blacks kept at the farm at Benson long after the need for them had passed. The blacks were dangerous and hard to control. They were also beautiful and challenging, a symbol of the romantic early days of farming when horses and men worked dawn to dusk together.

Don's boyhood affection for horses made me feel a fondness for them, too. During our college days Don sometimes took me, freshly outfitted in tall riding boots and jodhpurs, to riding stables near the Cities. By the time we first visited his parents' farm near Benson, I felt a growing confidence around horses. As soon as we arrived we mounted up: Don on Ruby, a tired, white horse belonging to the hired man, and I on Don's beloved Brownie, a horse half bronco and half Morgan. As if he knew I was timid and inexperienced, Brownie performed as decorously as his nature allowed. His faultless behavior was reinforced by two things. Don had harnessed him with a check bit and a Western saddle, and he and Ruby never left my side. Later, when it was time for Don to help with chores, I begged to take Brownie alone. He finally agreed, not wanting to destroy my budding courage.

Riding alone was wonderful and exhilarating; the horse's cantering gait was smooth, swift, thrilling. All went well until we turned toward home. Little did I know how a horse's enthusiasm for feed and stall could add fleetness to his feet. Nor did I realize that my efforts to control him soon flipped the bit so that it didn't curb him at all. He reached his full gallop in a few bounds, and my terrified screams only made him stretch out his neck, lay back his ears, and fly. My head scarf and pins let go, and my long hair streamed behind me as we approached the double turn at the wooden bridge. I never expected to negotiate that turn, and forgetting my pride, I grabbed the saddle horn and clung desperately. Oh, how I clung!

The horse kept his footing, crossed the bridge, and gained still more speed in the long straightaway to the old Douglas home. Two tall, iron gateposts guarded the driveway, each topped with an ornamental spike. I had barely noticed them as I rode out, but now they rose up ominous and threatening. To make a right-angle turn between them was obviously beyond my powers. My overactive imagination supplied a shocking picture of my body hurtling through the air, as if drawn by a magnet, impaling itself on a spike, and twisting there like a weathervane in the wind. Then mysteriously, mercifully, Brownie's speed slackened. As we came up the lane, Brownie had subsided to a fast walk. I understood why when I saw Don and his mother running to the barn lot gate. They had heard the horse's pounding hoofbeats and knew Brownie would never slow up unless he saw his master.

Suddenly weak and trembling, I slipped gratefully into Don's arms. His mother said he was paler than I. The fingernails on my right hand were bent clear back upon themselves from gripping the saddle. We joked that with a grip like that, Brownie could not have lost me no matter what he did.

Later I discovered that Don let the horse run full tilt to the barn lot and skid to a stop while Don vaulted lightly over the gate and then opened it to let the horse through. The barn door was kept closed. Otherwise, if Brownie found the first gate open, he would streak across the lot and run into the barn, trusting his rider to duck to avoid decapitation at the entrance.

On our Appleton farm, Ranger, Papa's big black gelding, was the only riding horse. When we moved to the farm, I was told that his Roman nose was a sign of a stubborn, morose disposition. With Papa on his back, his behavior was sedate and predictable. They made a companionable pair as they headed off to check the cattle in the pasture—the big, heavy man confidently sitting astride the big, plodding horse. Papa sometimes had to dismount to fix a fence or to examine a feeder calf; he had taught Ranger to let himself be led to a rock where he stood quietly while Papa stepped up to hoist himself back into the saddle.

When we later rented a part of that pasture to a young couple whose two Shetland ponies had colts within a few days of each other, our children were impatient to see them. On a lovely Sunday afternoon in about 1955, when a friend with her two young girls was visiting from New Jersey, we all trooped to the nearby farm. We found our neighbors already in the yard enjoying the antics of their colts. As most farm people do, our neighbors took much pleasure in baby animals. We joined them at the yard fence only twenty feet or so from the ponies and their mothers. Ours and our friend's children lined up, their faces bright and their chatter temporarily silenced by their awe at the tiny, perfect, beautiful creatures.

The colts frisked about, their legs with the knobby knees amazingly steady after only about a week of life. At first they stayed close to their mothers and only occasionally gave a practice leap. Soon they showed their interest in us by tossing their heads, pricking their ears forward, kicking up their hooves, and whisking their short tails. We looked for distinctive markings, but their coats were a plain dusky chestnut. Their dark eyes gleamed enormous as they gained courage and cavorted closer to investigate us.

Bruce cried, "Look, Mom, that one wants to tell us something!"

Indeed it did look as if they wanted to get acquainted. At the sound of Bruce's voice, however, they wheeled around and bobbed back to their mothers.

Before we knew it, they looked as if they were daring each other to run past us and then back to their mothers in a big circle. Round and round they went. We adults were as delighted as the children with the graceful, joyous performance.

All at once the leader slipped. His small hooves simply could not keep up to the momentum of his body. He went down hard onto his side, and we heard a heavy grunt. He hoisted himself up hurriedly, first shoulder, then body, as if to make believe it hadn't happened at all. Then, overcome with shame, he bent his head down and, with tail pressed against his retreating rear, slipped quickly over to his mother and ducked out of sight behind her.

It was so human, so irresistibly funny, that we all started laughing. Adult and child alike could remember all too well times when our confidence had outrun our skill. We longed to comfort the crestfallen colt.

Bruce asked, "Is he crying, Mom?" and just then he got his answer. The cocky baby Shetland peeped out around his mother and looked at us as if to say, "Are you still watching me?"

We were and we did, for quite a while longer, but the magic of the moment was gone. The little horses looked tired after their exertions, as well they might.

For the children it was total love. Actual ownership was

irrelevant. Long after the babies were grown, they were still referred to as "our baby colts," bonded in a way even their own pony and later their riding horse could not match.

When Anne's pony, King, arrived, she and Billy lost interest in big horses. After King came Rabbit. Rabbit had her name when we purchased her, a gentle chestnut mare who had been trained to race as a trotter but was not fast enough. The name apparently was a slur on her fleetness.

Don and I, however, soon had every reason to think well of her. One bright day while we were having morning coffee on the back steps, twelve-year-old Anne rode Rabbit through the wide stock gate into the dooryard. She called out to us as she passed, then turned down the sidewalk that led out to the lane. Four-year-old Bruce fell in behind them on his tricycle, and Spike, the big German shepherd, came rollicking up alongside and ran ahead of Bruce. Anne led off in a half-trot down the sidewalk between the garage close on the left and the huge lilac bush that crowded in on the right. Spike, looking backwards at Bruce and barking excitedly, overtook them and found himself unexpectedly between Rabbit's legs. The horse stopped abruptly, trembling. The trike caught up and actually struck Rabbit's hind legs just as the dog spurted out between her front legs. The horse squatted back. Don and I started up and watched helplessly. Everything a horse instinctively hates—the small, closed-in space, the unseen tricycle nudging her from behind, the noise of the child and the dog—made a perfect setup for a tragic accident. If Rabbit kicked, Bruce would almost certainly be struck. If she bucked, Anne would land on the concrete. We did not dare call out or run to them lest we precipitate our worst fears.

Breathlessly we watched. The dog sprang forward, glad to be out of reach of those hooves. Rabbit picked her way past the overhanging bush and waited motionless while Anne leaned to unlock the narrow gate, then bounded ahead. Not until then did she buck. Anne, thinking the emergency had passed, was unprepared and landed painfully in a burdock thistle. Understandably, she was furious. Bruce hurried up solemn-eyed with sympathy for his sister, blissfully unaware of the danger he had been in.

As we now dashed to help, Don marveled out loud how horses seem to sense the helplessness of children and protect them. I looked at him in grateful agreement. Today it had real meaning for me. Now I owed my children's safety to this "dumb" animal. Still holding our shaken-up daughter, I freed an arm to pet Rabbit's neck. Pulling the horse's head close, I felt a bond and a sharing that was new to me.

Harvest

Driving sheep from Appleton

Overleaf:
Anne and a Shetland colt, with Bill, Don, Marjorie, and Bruce

Ewe Children

Don's rangy, fun-loving friend, Art Sackreiter, ran the co-op grain elevator in nearby Milan and made it worth our while to move our grain through him. Don said we never got the top dollar on the market, but we always got close to it.

Just once, though, Art made a mistake—and a bad one. He invested in a flock of one hundred Hampshire sheep and placed them on shares with a farmer who then moved to Minnesota's north woods, taking the flock with him. The usual arrangement is for the owner to get half the wool clip and half the lambs, but for three years Art received nothing. The renter had no phone; letters went unanswered. Because Art's duties at the elevator never let up, he had no chance to get away to see what was happening.

One morning in April 1954, Art pulled into the yard in a vast semitrailer truck and began to work on Don in his sidelong indirect way to go with him to repossess the sheep. Don protested with his work: his planter still lacked a final adjustment and timing; the fuel injector for the M tractor needed his personal attention.

"But where did you get the semi?" he asked.

Art laughed. "Remember that independent trucker from Dawson? He drove in with this semi and unloaded his grain and began yelling like usual, 'I'm sick of this job. I'd like to go fishing and forget all about it.'

"'Well, do it!' I said. 'Take my car, and go fishing, and I'll take your semi and reclaim my sheep!'"

The trucker eagerly agreed, so early Saturday morning Art was standing in our driveway with the children running out to see what was going on. At twelve, Anne was impulsive and capable; Bill, at nine, was easygoing and a natural with machinery; and Bruce at three was all blue eyes under the bobbing ball fringe of his Mexican hat.

When he realized that Don was really refusing to accompany him, Art admitted he did not know how to turn the ungainly thing around. He sounded forlorn as he said he'd have to go on alone. Don climbed in, pulled the big rig farther into the driveway, and maneuvered it into position. I didn't really know until afterward that Don had never driven a semi before. Perhaps Art was sly enough to get him behind the wheel on purpose, counting on the thrill to help persuade him to go along. It always surprised me that Art himself had little skill as an operator of big machinery, and I could see that Don felt concern for him. (I don't doubt that our friend had figured on this, too.)

Don did agree to go, and as soon as that was decided, Art began trying to interest him in taking the sheep on shares. Don flatly refused, saying he did not want any more stock.

"You have room for them, don't you, on your river pasture or the small pasture? It's a shame for rich meadow like that to go to waste."

"I don't want them, Art. Planting will start next week, and I've got to get four hundred acres of corn in and another four hundred of soybeans."

"I'll give you easy terms, and these ewes are young sound Hamps," he urged.

"Cash is short right now, and there's gas and seed and fertilizer and wages, and it's a long time till harvest. No sheep. And that's final!"

It was late afternoon before they found the right village. They finally located the renter's place far out in the woods. Apparently no one was at home, so the weary men used the well-trained stock dog and rounded up the sheep into the dooryard. Just then the wife turned up. As she came toward them, she gave a hand signal, and the waiting dog burst into action, scattering the animals in every direction. Her silent, stooped husband appeared, and Art told them to have the sheep in the lot early next morning or he would call the sheriff.

On the next day they sorted off all the ewes, then added ewe lambs to make up for the ones that had died or been sold. Generously, Art gave a share of the remaining lambs to the couple so they could build up a bunch of their own.

When they were nearly home, Art asked Don what the flock was worth. Don knew the sheep market. He calculated a moment and named a good figure. They had been well cared for and had no doubt produced a handsome income for the thieving farmer. Again Art wheedled Don to buy the sheep. When Don still refused, Art confessed that he had no place to put them. He begged for temporary pasture. That changed everything, and Don readily granted permission, helping out a neighbor as farmers traditionally do. Then Art made a final proposition that Don could not refuse.

"Buy them for your children. Nothing down. Let the kids pay for the flock out of their share of the wool and lambs, and there'll be no interest on the principal. You'll be doing me a big favor."

How could a father refuse?

Now Art had what he had been cleverly angling for since he had driven over the previous morning, and the children had a project of their own.

High Expectations and a Ha-Ha

One hundred hungry, wooly helpers!" I exulted the next morning when the sheep were waiting to be turned out into the Big Yard to mow nearly seven acres. Bill and Anne and Bruce were all puffed up with importance as they began their new shepherding duties with zest. The sun glinted on their yellow curls as the future farmers crossed the main driveway that connected the granary and Papa's house on the west to the two red barns on the east. Farther to the east were the shelters for hogs and cattle and the feed lots, where at present the sheep were penned.

The children stationed themselves by the garden's woven-wire fence, intent on protecting "Mother's vegetables." They stood about halfway between the houses, near the pump and stock tank. Beyond the driveway and the Milwaukee tracks lay the bulk of the cropland. The spur track, which had served this stock farm early in the century, had been removed. By the time of our sheep venture, we used truckers to carry most of our stock to the yards at South St. Paul. The pasture where the sheep would later graze stretched south of the buildings nearly a mile to the Pomme de Terre River.

Although Don never wanted me to help in the field, I had learned to manage the walking power mower. Even with that, the grass often got ahead of me while I tended to house, meals, and garden and taxied the kids to piano and swimming lessons. Now I was sure that never again would I spend hours trudging up and down behind that noisy mower.

The morning was cool and faultless as I stood on the kitchen steps and watched Don open the gates. The pretty little Hampshires, with their shiny black faces and legs, flowed slowly out. My delight turned to a sinking feeling as I saw them spread in every direction like slippery grain spilling onto the concrete granary floor. They paid no attention to the grass but began to nibble on fruit trees and bushes. Don hurried to protect the young cherry trees, and I ran in the opposite direction to the raspberry patch. Everywhere I looked there was a pulsing gray ocean of sheep and more sheep.

At that time we had never seen the ha-has of the English country estates. Ha-has, sunken fences or escarpments built into a ditch or ravine, prevented animals from escaping and reaching an estate lawn and gardens. The lords and ladies could see the sheep picturesquely grazing the hillsides, apparently roaming free, for the ha-ha is hidden. Because our land was almost as flat as the South Dakota plains, which were only twenty-five miles west of us, a ha-ha would not have been practical to build.

I watched in bewilderment as the flock continued to disperse. We would have to do something to control them—but what? Could we use movable brush barriers as the Basques did? Thank goodness we didn't depend on great stone fences like those on the island of Crete. As I dashed from the raspberry patch to the peony bushes, I pictured having to roam forever with the sheep, as shepherds in the West or in the Scottish Highlands did. There they control vast bands with a system of rhythmic commands to their sheep dogs.

We had felt secure with our fence around the garden, but it immediately proved inadequate. The children looked like ill-assorted cheerleaders as they doffed their jackets and waved them to scare the less timid sheep away from the lettuce and carrots. What was the matter? How could the sheep's first choice, after the garden, be berry bushes or an occasional weed in the ditches? Perversely, they moseyed in every direction until we were grateful for the cattle guard that prevented their crossing the railroad tracks and the busy highway. They spread into the grove. Some bobbed along in the ditches. One led a procession behind the garage. And they ignored the great expanse of lawn. We soon felt as if we were experiencing a ha-ha of a different kind, and this time the joke was on us.

We all pitched in. Anne and Bill had an exhausting morning chasing the sheep and gradually learning to let the animals forage at will—unless they trespassed on garden or flowering plants. Bruce had tagged along valiantly until his enthusiasm and his short legs were used up. He joined Don and me as dinner time approached, and we returned toward the house.

Then I noticed a plump ewe leading a band toward the open stock gate of our dooryard. We quietly slipped inside to observe. They ignored the buckthorn hedge and approached the lemon-scented, white lilacs with their double florets. I held my breath, for those lilacs in the moonlight held romantic memories of moments that Don and I had spent there. But the sheep pushed past them and past that perfectly proportioned buckeye tree, which won my heart my first year on the farm. As I watched for the sheep's next move, I was glad only a few had come inside the enclosure to threaten what for me was an oasis nestled in this hot, dusty farm. Even the prairie winds didn't dry it out. Satisfied at last that they had located the most tender morsels, the sheep began to attack the flowers, still ignoring the grass. That did it! Quickly my husband and I began to herd them out of our little sanctuary. Suddenly I stopped and stared at one of the sheep.

"There's old Miss Blandby! There she is!" I shrieked. My husband looked around questioningly and found me studying a faded-looking ewe, whose head drooped and limp ears folded down.

"You never met her—she was a volunteer—at the hospital." Gusts of laughter took my breath, and I leaned weakly against the fence. "Kind, gentle, but always sorrowful. Even her smile was sad. This ewe's a dead ringer!"

Don had to chase the sheep back out into the Big Yard alone and secure the gate, for I was still giggling uncontrollably. "And to think I said all sheep looked alike."

Our next surprise late that afternoon was a welcome one. We saw a lively little ewe taste the "lamb's quarters" with apparent relish, then the dandelions, then the tall horse weeds. Soon all the sheep began to demolish any and every kind of weed. One even stretched up on hind legs to nip off the purple flower of the hated Scotch thistle. The animals scattered and devoured with gusto. As we watched, they began to graze the grass. By the end of the week we found that the unpredictable lawnmowers had manicured the grounds. The fence-rows and wood-lot had never been as clean, the grass was neat and trim, we had a rest from mowing, and we found ourselves enjoying the presence of the gentle animals. It was a relief when they were turned out to pasture, however, and we no longer had to lock gates every time we ventured in and out of the yard.

"Will they ever learn, Dad?" Bill asked. "Anne and Brucie and I tried to teach them not to eat the peonies and carrots and fruit trees."

"I kept telling that little one, and she wouldn't listen," Bruce put in earnestly.

"I'm afraid not, boys. Even that pompous one you think looks like your school principal, Bill, is just a sheep. Sheep don't learn to get along with people. People learn to get along with sheep."

And Don was right. When the newness wore off, the sheep got their mowing job done in three days instead of a week. The children monitored them faithfully and enjoyed discovering individual sheep who resembled acquaintances. When the sheep were in the Big Yard, I got used to people coming into the kitchen laughing. Don even announced one time, "Today I found our preacher."

Once he had pointed out the resemblance, I couldn't believe I hadn't seen it before—the stiffly held head, the deliberate, careful progress, the eyes that seemed to take your measure. Now I think of these look-alike sheep as ha-has.

Don at the controls of his combine

A Rube Goldberg
Contraption and
an Accident

In late July of the first summer the children owned the sheep, college friends drove out from the Twin Cities for their first visit to the farm. The Clarkes arrived at noon one breathless Sunday with their dark-eyed daughter CC. Happy to be together, we sat down to a roast beef dinner with new potatoes and the first sweet corn of the season. This year we had triumphed in the perennial contest with a raccoon who liked to climb and break the cornstalks, neatly peel back the husks, and nibble the tender kernels that were not yet mature enough for our taste. The salvaged corn tasted doubly delicious, and as we ate we began to feel as carefree as in our school days. Except for the oppressive heat, we could think of nothing that could cloud the pleasure of the day. Nivea had news of classmates, and we lingered chatting over the lemon pie and coffee. The children hurried off to pet the rabbits and hunt the new kittens.

The previous week we had purchased our first self-propelled combine, a twelve-foot Cockshutt. It was a marvelous, intricate machine that allowed Don to cut his crop, thresh it, and return the straw as mulch to help hold water in our soil and prevent wind erosion—all in one pass. We could not have been prouder of this machine if we ourselves had fashioned it. Large machinery was becoming a necessity on farms as big as ours. Owning a combine assured Don of harvesting his crop at its prime. He arranged to combine for other farmers as well and so bring in extra income. It was a considerable investment for us, but I understood it meant flexibility, speed, and efficiency in harvesting crops. I also think it carried a certain status for Don. Big machinery was becoming the dividing line between financial success and mere maintenance; it also called for bigger tracts of land. Ours was already one of the largest in the countryside, but Don often rented additional acres.

Almost as eager as the children, we led our guests out to the barn driveway where the combine stood, blindingly reflecting the midday sunlight from its resplendent orange paint. This invention can be described as a machine turned inside out with the levers, handles, belts, augurs, and cutting bars on the outside. A car with no body might be comparable, except that its only purpose is locomotion. A combine, however, is just that—a combination of all possible functions at once. Don frequently said that he used his knees, both hands, and feet to operate it, and he still needed a tail.

Our friends walked clear around our new prize. They frowned in concentration. They shook their heads. Romeyn's expression was puzzled as he laid his hand gingerly on a narrow black belt that looped up over a pulley. He followed it with his fingers to where it disappeared into the machine's interior. Seeing us look quizzically at him, he exclaimed with feeling, "Boy! Talk about a Rube Goldberg contraption!"

This reflected none of the envy of our farm friends, and we were unreasonably disappointed—perhaps partly because the comparison was so apt. In a moment of embarrassed silence we heard the afternoon passenger train approaching rapidly. A long chilling steam whistle sounded. Brakes screeched, followed by an alarming cacophony of toots and whistles. Then the train picked up speed again and was gone.

"The children?" We had been so absorbed in our new machine I had temporarily lost track of their whereabouts. But immediately all four came running. They followed Don to the railroad near the woodlot. There sixteen sheep lay dead and bleeding. Two more had to be shot. CC and Bruce were persuaded to return to the house with CC's mother. Anne cried at first with anger and shock at the carnage. Then she and Bill gamely helped with rounding up the uninjured animals and getting them back into the yard. While he said little, Bill's blue eyes looked purple—the way they always were when he was distressed.

Our friends' initiation to the farm had been more than anyone had bargained for. The question of financial loss had not occurred to the children, and, in fact, it was slight. The sheep had escaped onto the tracks through a break in the railroad fence. After the company inspected and repaired it, we eventually received a check to cover the loss.

Each of the children sought reassurance after the guests had left. Anne, practical and direct, wanted to know how we could have prevented the accident. Bill just needed to cling a little, without any words. With tears in his eyes, Bruce knew that he would miss his friends—

especially one of the newborn lambs. This lamb's tail circled so wildly when he dropped onto his front knees to nurse that Don said he looked like a helicopter. After that, Bruce watched and watched as if he expected to see the little lamb airborne. Now, experiencing his first loss, he moaned, "I know I'll never have another pet like Whirley Bird."

Papa Advises One Last Time

B ucks are half the flock, Don," Papa had advised in 1954, as we started the sheep venture. "Buy the best." Papa, as usual, expected no argument. He leaned his elbows on the table in the cheery kitchen and rubbed his thick, muscular hands together. "I've been through it," he insisted, "and my experience with sheep says you always buy quality."

Don, eager for his afternoon lunch, pulled up a chair. A cold October rain was falling. His father had come over to help with repairing the corn picker in the unheated shop, and now they welcomed the warmth from the oven's open door. The cheerful Red Wing pottery glowed bright as I filled the cups with clear, egg coffee "like Mother Douglas used to make."

As I busied myself with serving the pie, I looked at Papa's large frame and tried to imagine him as a young man. I'd heard him tell many times of the twenty-three cousins he had organized to form a great checkerboard of homestead claims, stretching into South Dakota. All but Papa and two others, however, were scared off by the danger of Indian hostilities. At the turn of the century,

Papa Douglas, second from left, as a young homesteader with his cousins and neighboring rancher

the memory of Custer and the Little Bighorn was still fresh.

After proving his claim, Papa sold it to pay for education and apprenticeship as a lawyer; then he married and eventually built a fine house on the big farm he bought in Iowa. At the same time, he satisfied his wanderlust with a gold-mining fling in British Columbia. Later he turned down an invitation to run for senator because he would not agree to follow the strict Democratic party line. About this time he moved into semiretirement at Lake Minnewashta, where Don and Glenn spent their late grade-school years. What a shock it must have been for this family, too, to give up their comfortable home and move to the inconveniences of a farmhouse where you carried all the water in and out. Where you did your part in a daily grind of taxing physical labor—always at the mercy of the weather.

I had always thought Don's good looks reflected his mother's small regular features and poised bearing. Yet she, like me a slender five feet six inches, was a foot shorter than he. Today, as I watched the two men together, I realized that his father's decisiveness and commanding manner were echoed in the son's confident approach to living.

"I've just been reading about Rambouillet sheep," I offered as I laid the mail on the table and followed it with plates of hot apple pie and hunks of pungent blue cheese. "They're bigger, and they grow faster, according to your farm paper."

"Yes, developed from a cross—a newer breed—but not for Minnesota," Papa elaborated. "I've seen them out West, as well as the white-faced Suffolk and the Shropshires. Black-faced Shropshires! Now that's a fine breed—medium-sized, prolific, adaptable. Get Shrops, Don."

Before Don could answer, I began to laugh. "Wasn't that a Shropshire buck that Mother Douglas always told about? Remember? 'Nothing but trouble,' she'd say. 'No fence was high enough, and lambs he sired came too early and continued coming all spring.' She told it as if most of them ended up as orphans in her kitchen. She always joked that she'd never forget Lem."

"That's right," Papa grinned at me. "We called him Lem after that county commissioner in town who got around a good deal in unexpected places."

"And the ladies all liked him, I hear." Don laughed, too, having heard the gossip.

As I refilled the cups, the aroma brought to mind a vivid image of Mother Douglas. I could see her cheeks, so fresh and unwrinkled, and the soft hair that had turned white in her thirties—as Don's was beginning to do.

Don returned to his father's dictum. "No. No Shropshires for me, Dad. I've considered Columbias. They're a newer large breed. But the Columbia lambs might be too big for our Hamp ewes if I decide to cross-breed. And the co-op man says the Columbia fleece is not so heavy."

"I'd agree with you there," the older man nodded. "But you've got to decide, Son. Your bucks should be with the flock now if you want to command the markup for lamb in the Easter and Passover trade. Five months from middle October is middle March and, at one year old, your lamb becomes mutton. Sell all your castrated buck lambs a year from March, and you'll probably get twenty-five cents more per hundred pounds for them. You'll be keeping the ewe lambs, of course, to build the flock. Get Shrop bucks, Son. You won't be sorry."

"Sure, I'll be keeping the ewe lambs, Dad, but I guess I've already decided about the bucks. I have a chance to pick up four registered Hampshire bucks tomorrow. As soon as I get them home, I'll turn them in with the flock. They are fine young bucks. Not too different from Shropshires, really."

Don valued his father's advice, but after more than ten years of total partnership, he now kept the children's project entirely separate and felt free to make his decision independently. He was putting himself firmly in charge. I was glad Don had decided to stick with the sturdy, gentle Hampshire stock. I'd been told they often had twins with pretty markings of neat black stockings and shiny black faces contrasting with heavy gray wool.

"You must plan to sell them at the end of the season," said Papa. "You don't want to take any chance of having your bucks breeding their own issue. You have to begin right away to watch for some new proven ones for next season. Always buy quality."

I had already discovered that sheep raising was not simple. However, listening to Papa's talk always gave me some clues to this unpredictable business. I also understood more about my father-in-law and could now link him to an early photo as William Stephen A. Douglas, the dashing homesteader, with a jaunty cowboy hat and ready rifle.

The late afternoon sunshine startled me when it glimmered across the table. The sky was clearing. Don reached for his damp denim jacket. His father reluctantly struggled into his, too, and did I just imagine that he looked back with longing at the remainder of the pie? Chore time again, and time for me to call for the children at their friend's home in town, and get busy with supper. I, too, rose reluctantly. I had half expected a fresh story to be dredged up from the old man's rich and detailed memory. I suspected that if the rain had gone on, so would Papa. Of course, I again agonized over the way he had slipped back into treating Don like a boy, although in the dozen-plus years we had been here, Don had gradually taken over most of the management. He bought and sold livestock, planned crop rotation, handled the purchase of machinery, did all hiring. Now we were buying Papa out. We were dreaming more and more of the time we could sell out and return to our interrupted life in the Cities. Only Don's filial loyalty and his sunny disposition kept things fairly calm.

The screen door banged behind the men, and Papa's voice floated back. "Now you check and be sure those bucks are registered stock. They are half the flock, you know. You'd do better with Shropshires if you want my advice, and—Shrops—Shrops—"

That quiet afternoon is happily remembered now, for it was followed by a shocking day later that same month. The older children were at school, Don and a new man were in the field, and Bruce was building a tottering silo of red and white blocks under the kitchen table while I cleaned beets for pickles.

Our friend Skinny Anderson from the furniture store drove into the yard. He had been making a delivery when he saw Papa's tractor across the field, south of the highway. It had stopped while pushing at the fence till it ran out of gas. Papa was cupped securely in the seat but was slumped over the steering wheel, apparently felled by a final heart attack. Skinny had determined that it was too late for help; he told me to go at once with a pillow to put under Papa's head to prevent his face from being disfigured as it rested on the steering wheel. He would get help and return later with a doctor.

I nodded. My mind seemed to separate from my body. While my hands tucked a pillow into a fresh slip, I was imagining Papa's Vivian long ago raising the Eider geese and plucking their down to stuff that very pillow. My feet carried me to find the car keys, but I was seeing Papa on the day he borrowed that car to drive to Benson for his second marriage. I heard my own voice explaining to Bruce, as if it came from far away—like Papa's voice in that dream about the lumber pile. I was swallowed up in memories of this man who had once been such a disturbing influence in my life.

As we eased from the highway to the little gravel road leading to the river, we could see the man and tractor alike spent and silent. I cringed at the thought of the strange task ahead of me, as I struggled across the stubbly field, pillow clutched in my arms and big-eyed child following. A belated flood of tenderness washed over me as I moved Papa's heavy head barely enough to squeeze the pillow under the lifeless cheek.

Florence was away visiting one of her sons, and Papa's small home seemed lonely and remote from our sunny pasture and the animals there. How had he felt about it? Was he ready to go? I wondered. His life had surely been full. As he started his tractor that morning, his eyes may have rested on his half-dozen steers or the last tomatoes in his little garden patch. Or on his prize possession—the artesian well that tapped the level of water the driller had not been able to reach for us.

"Oh, Papa, I hope you found happiness here. I didn't always understand you, and I did get mad sometimes, but we'll miss you. We'll never forget. . . ."

I heard a voice. In the rush of feelings I had momentarily forgotten Bruce standing bewildered beside me.

"Mama, what's the matter, Mama? Why won't Papa answer you? Tell him to wake up."

Tears overflowed, and his arms grabbed me tight as I leaned and scooped him up.

"He always tells me a story. I want him to tell me a story," he sobbed. I must have been lost in memories longer than I realized.

I saw Skinny's truck turning from the highway. I needed to get to the field and find Don.

"Say good-bye, Darling. Say good-bye for now to Papa. He can't tell you stories anymore, but you and I will always remember those stories, won't we? And we'll never, never, ever forget Papa."

Easter Bottle Baby

After Papa's death, Don wasted no time in seeking a sale and almost at once found two promising leads. They needed the bank's backing, of course, but as Easter approached his talk was full of happy possibilities. I hoped that Papa had felt some pride—some gratitude even—at the way his son ran the farm. As far as I know he never expressed such feelings to Don.

Don was content, however. Papa had made financial arrangements before his second marriage and his move to the small farm acreage that we had once rented to the owners of the ponies. Florence moved back to Benson to be near her family and friends. Papa had willed his small farm to Don's brother Glenn, and he forgave the remainder of what we owed him on the ranch.

That Easter, the children and I looked forward to lambing. We pictured cuddly little Easter card creatures gamboling about in the sunshine. In reality, some were born as early as February, when even the sunny days were cold. Some came in frigid rains or in March snowstorms. Many came into our kitchen chilled and wet and dirty, needing to be warmed near the oven, rubbed with a towel, and bottle-fed before being returned to their

*Bruce with Baabaa,
1958*

mothers in the sheds. First-time mothers sometimes had to be helped to claim their young by being penned together in close quarters to enforce bonding. Once a lamb had nursed, it could safely be removed to the kitchen for a short time without endangering family ties.

Only one lamb that first season was permanently abandoned. What pride I felt as that bedraggled, skinny creature began to respond to the warmth and the feedings. She stood on her blanket in her carton and butted and wriggled with joy as she drank. Her tail, which would later be docked, rotated rapidly in total bliss. It looked like a crank that powered the feeding process, and it scarcely missed a beat.

Total involvement with one lamb, however, can be tiresome. Worse yet, Baabaa strongly resented being returned to the shed. By Easter, which came nearly mid-April that year, she was a husky animal of thirty-five pounds and looked much larger with her curly, gray coat and black face. Easter Sunday dawned dreary and wet after several days of rain, and the feed lot was hopelessly muddy. Don finished chores early, and the boys' faces shone above their blazers and Eton-collared shirts. Anne was radiant in the lacy red wool dress my mother had crocheted for her. Breakfast was cleaned up in short order, and the smell of beef roast already escaped the oven.

As Don pulled the car up to the nearest gate for us, I opened the door and turned to help Anne with the umbrella. Before we could take a breath, Baabaa had scrambled up the concrete steps and clattered into the kitchen. We never fed her inside anymore, but here she was, wet to the point of dripping, her fur matted with mud and straw. She skidded and slipped, her tiny hooves making grubby streaks across the shiny linoleum. She bumped against the white enamel stove, leaving her imprint there in gray and black. Recognizing Anne, who had often fed her, the lamb lunged toward her, and Anne barely escaped with an agile leap to the corner.

"Open the door!" I yelled. Bruce and Bill and I tried to shoo the befuddled beast out without touching her, but again and again she stubbornly dashed and skidded in the wrong direction. Visions of filthy hands and ruined clothing replaced white lilies and Easter music in my mind as time kept slipping by in this ridiculous performance.

Don was unaware of our plight. We heard his tap on the horn, reminding us that he was due in the choir. Time was growing short. In desperation, I grabbed deeply into the nasty, smelly, wet wool, trying to keep myself clear of the lamb as I pushed and pulled. Somehow, I maneuvered the determined animal out onto the stoop and down the steps. I hung on while the children made their getaway. A quick handwash and we were in the car without any visible sign of our adventure, although I could detect a faint skunklike aroma even through my best white kid gloves. As we drove off, Don had the courage to joke that he would have to count heads when his family came out of the house after this to be sure just what he let into the car.

No Place for a Sheep-Killin' Dog

L iving at Appleton near the clear Pomme de Terre River, we learned over the years to expect hazards. In dry summers deer might ravage a cornfield. Coyotes occasionally appeared from nowhere hunting a lamb, and often dogs—alone or in small marauding packs—used darkness to cover their gruesome sport with the sheep.

One day at dinner, ten-year-old Bill was remembering such tales. "Tell about the sheep killin' dog, Dad. There's still time for nooning, isn't there?" he coaxed.

We all sat in various stages of weariness around the ravaged dinner table. By noon, we had already put in a long day in the heat. Enoch Bagstad, uncle of Don's brother's wife, was our hired hand that summer. We enjoyed his Norwegian brogue and were used to his tough, wiry figure never hurrying at chores and apparently never tiring. Heikke Wagner, a town mechanic, was helping that week, too. He was making adjustments on the caterpillar tractor, which all the men hated and hoped we could sell. Heikke had uncanny skill with machinery, but I used to tease him that he needed coffee breaks more often than our son, Bruce, ever needed his bottle. David, the teen-aged son of the Cairnses', was also helping that year when his father could spare him. A slender, quiet boy, he had pushed back his chair and sprawled there enjoying the talk.

Anne, now nearly thirteen, sometimes left the dinner table for her book or piano when she had finished her meal, but today she was drinking in praise for her crusty oatmeal bread and the fresh fried potatoes she had made with her special chopper. But Bill always loved to be with the men, and now he took advantage of a break in the talk to ask for one of his favorite stories.

"Please, Dad? That mean dog that sneaked out on dark nights and never got caught! Tell that one!"

The men, seeing Don's indulgent look, held up their cups for more coffee. They welcomed a chance to rest a bit longer from haying in the hot sun. I set the coffeepot on the table and went to retrieve Bruce, who was waking from a morning nap. I settled him in his high chair where he smiled and chattered to David, who helped him with his dinner.

Don began with his usual relish for a good yarn.

"Before your mother and I moved to the farm, when we both had jobs in the Cities, I used to have sheep out on shares with several farmers who wanted to get a start that way. When I stopped in one Saturday at Joe's place to check on his bunch, he told me he had a bad break. A dog got into his flock one night. While he heard the com-motion and ran out, he didn't catch sight of the invader. He found two sheep dead and three so badly torn they had to be destroyed."

"Nothing to do but kill the attacker," Enoch volunteered in his singsong Scandinavian lilt. "They never quit killin' once they start the bloody sport."

"Right," Don answered. "Only problem was we had to catch him first. Such dogs know that they're doing wrong, and they get mighty crafty at covering their tracks."

"Dogs are smart." This was young Bill. "Spike can think just like people."

"This Joe-fellah didn't know whose dog it was?" Enoch asked as he pulled another cigarette from the package Don had purchased for him that morning. The expense of three packs for thirty-five cents, together with his Saturday night "draws," was tallied against his salary. It had been raised April 1 from winter pay of $50 to $112.50 a month—plus housing, food, and laundry. Don always paid good wages and promptly.

"No, he hadn't seen it," Don replied. "It was spring and the snow was almost gone, and he found only a couple of paw marks. Thought it was a big dog, but couldn't find the trail. I had an idea how devious they could be, so I had better luck."

"And you really know how to track a critter!" Bill had witnessed his father's skill.

"You know a thing or two yourself, Bill. You can tell the way the paw marks point, and whether they are far apart and dug in to show the animal is running. But mostly a person gets to know what to expect, I guess. Anyway, the few prints in snow or mud led unmistakably one and a half miles due north, then a mile east, a mile and a half south and, finally, right into a farm dooryard."

"Just a mile from where you started then, huh, Dad?"

"Right, Son. Now are you going to let me tell this story or not?"

Bill knew the best part was coming and waited in anticipation.

"I was lucky. A shepherd-type dog barked as I came in, and the owner promptly came to the dooryard and called him to heel. When the farmer learned my business, he gathered that big dog up in his arms like a baby, looked me right in the eye, and swore his dog had never even chased a cat. I described my tracking and offered to take him back to see the evidence. He flatly refused. Said his dog had been in the barn every night for three weeks. My eye lit on the dog's chest. I showed the farmer the dried blood that still clung to the fur. There was even sheep's wool in that dog's teeth, and still the man stubbornly refused to admit the truth. No way could I separate dog and man, and I couldn't really shoot both of 'em, now could I?

"I went to the neighboring farm where my longtime friend Wayne Ricke lived. Like you said, Enoch, and like all stockmen from the days of the Wild West on, he agreed that a sheep-killin' dog must die.

"We went over every detail of my tracking, and he agreed fully with my judgment that his neighbor had a sheep-killin' dog. A wordless compact formed between us.

"Two weeks later—almost to the day—I received a postcard in the mail with no salutation and no signature. It said only, 'My neighbor does *not* have a sheep-killin' dog.'"

The men laughed, and he added, "Now if we don't get to work, the cattle won't have any hay this winter."

It was good, I guess, that the children had tales like this in their minds and understood that on a farm even pets have to mind the rules. Spike, as a just-weaned German

Bruce holds Spike as puppy, summer 1954

Spike teases Bruce, winter 1955

Bruce learns to play with Spike, spring 1955

shepherd puppy, had joined our family when Bruce was about three. The dog had never threatened anyone— even when Bruce found a clump of yellowish sand that he thought was a sweet parsnip, so plentiful that summer. Horrified, I saw him trying to force it down Spike's throat, saying, "Eat you' bah-snips. It's good for you!" By the time I reached him, Spike had wriggled away from Bruce's arms, and I wrapped my arms tight around the child. I marveled again at the forbearance animals seem to have with small children. And Bruce found better ways to play with Spike.

This dog never obeyed willingly, though. Nor did he learn to help with the stock. He seemed always to have an irrepressible flood of high spirits, and we all responded to his playfulness.

It came as a shock, then, to find a bloody scene one Sunday when Don and the older children went to check on the sheeps' water supply. Several sheep were torn and Spike was standing over a ewe with his teeth on her throat, growling as he slowly strangled her. As Don stepped in to stop him, Spike let the sheep's head drop from his muzzle, the hair on the back of his neck stood up, and he snarled at his master. As Don moved toward him, Spike finally crouched in submission.

The children stood frozen in horror and disbelief. Almost as sickened as they, Don sent Bill running to the house for the pistol and ammunition. He asked Anne if she would rather go back to the house than watch this grisly drama.

From nearby at the pump, Bruce and I heard what was happening, and I, too, tried to shepherd the children away, but all three were too involved with Spike to turn their backs. Reluctantly we all watched dry-eyed, but I felt physically ill. The dog and the injured sheep were killed quickly.

The sharp crack of the shots seemed to rivet us in our places and the silence echoed around us.

"I think he was playing," Anne finally ventured, sturdily defending him. "He was playing with the sheep and got rough and got too carried away."

"He wasn't a mean dog," Bill agreed, "till he saw the blood." Bill's voice quavered a bit, but he went on. "You remember what Enoch said—'once they start killing.'"

After a moment he continued more resolutely. "And we knew from the beginning a farmer has to protect his sheep."

Don's and my eyes met, but we said nothing. I felt Bruce pulling on my hand. "Why didn't Spike listen, Mom?"

"I'm sorry he didn't, Son," was all the comfort I could think of.

Again silence wrapped each of us in our separate thoughts. The children's pet—the children's sheep. It was heavy for them—for all of us.

Later that day, they bid farewell to their companion as they buried him under the big cottonwood. They were busy for a long time at the little mound there. They had parted with their pet, but they also parted that day with some of the innocence of childhood.

Don Encounters Problems

The children never tired of admiring the blocky black-faced ewes with their dainty wide-spread ears. Their favorites were Old Faithful and Big Mama—both of whom had twins year after year. One ewe twice had triplets, and she became known as the Great Earth Mother (GEM, or Gem, as we called her). The third year she produced only twins, and instead of delighting in her reduced burden, she adopted a lamb whose mother had not claimed him. Don was amazed because nature provides a ewe with accommodations for nursing only two. Gem managed to "eat for four" and to rotate feedings by gently kicking aside one baby after a feeding to take care of the third who nudged at her heels. Don slipped her a little extra feed when he could, but she was a loner and independent.

Almost as if it were a matter of pride, as well as obvious necessity, this ewe hunted her food in unexpected places—usually alone with her lambs. She worked along the fencerows where weeds grew up protected from the mower. When the corn and soybeans began to show through the black dirt, we all expected trouble and watched for her and her followers. She systematically tested the fences, and her determination was boundless.

Weeds in the west field got ahead of us one rainy year. Don hired a neighbor who owned a high boom to spray it. With the work finished, the men were enjoying coffee in our kitchen when Billy came running in, pointing and shouting that Gem was eating poison. Our problem ewe had sneaked under the barbed wire and was eating ravenously down the row. We all ran out to the field to chase her out to safety.

Secretly I admired this mother's cunning in caring for her family, until she overreached herself by interfering with my providing for mine. When she turned up in my garden, eating and trampling my prized Everbearing strawberries, my sentiments abruptly changed. I made such a fuss that the next day a beautiful, new, tightly woven wire fence—almost three feet high—surrounded my half acre of vegetables and berries. Late that afternoon, I found her happily surveying the culinary choices from inside the fence again. It had no break; she must have leapt it. There was no peace in the house until another width of woven wire was wrapped above the first on the tall metal fence posts. No known sheep could clear that bulwark. And none did.

The Great Earth Mother was a favorite subject of conversation. Don and I decided that had we been raising breeding stock, this ewe would have been prized as a strengthener of the breed. Soon we were laughing over her escapades, and I was pleased, for he had seemed depressed the last couple of days. I knew he was becoming concerned about his lack of progress with the only two leads he had found in trying to sell.

It was not until Don had finished supper one evening and the children were in bed that he finally told me the cause of his depression. He had learned at the bank that one potential buyer had withdrawn his offer angrily and refused to reconsider on any terms. The worst part was that a neighbor had deliberately given the man false information, fearing that if we sold out he would lose one of his main sources of bluegrass seed from our pasture.

Don had known it would not be easy to sell a big farm like ours, and he had been patient and thorough in making contacts and in advertising. Now he looked at me across the table, unable to hide the pain he felt. "Why do I keep thinking of our own dog Spike turning on me? Hacking up and baring his teeth? He'd known only love in this family."

"Don, who? Who could have wanted to do this to you?" I protested as I went to him.

"I'm not going to tell you, Marj. It won't help to have you carry that, too."

Characteristically, Don began aggressively seeking in other towns for backing for his one remaining prospect. He discovered a government support program for farmers and obtained an application form that he began to study.

Three Hunters

On Bill's thirteenth birthday in the summer of 1958, he was allowed to carry his grandfather's twelve-gauge shotgun. He had first fired it when he was eight. Then, in spite of careful coaching, its powerful recoil had knocked him flat. He had long known he was to inherit it, so he had learned how to clean the burned powder from the barrels and rub it with Hoppe's gun oil. (Just a whiff of the oil used to activate Papa's stories of fabled "snap" shots.) There were few chances that busy summer for hunting with his dad. However, pheasant season was another thing, and Bill's eagerness barely exceeded Don's.

As they started off together, I was impressed again with the many traits they shared, especially their transparent, unhesitating honesty and thoroughness. They both had a friendly, whole-hearted respect for another person, they loved a good story, they each had tenacity in mastering problems with machinery, and they could become totally involved in the hunt. I could see that this involvement helped to distract Don from the hateful news of his friend's betrayal.

That morning Bill proved to be similar in another way.

Bill, the hunter, with pheasants and fox, 1958

He had fast reflexes, and his father was delighted when he bagged two male ring-necked pheasants in quick succession. As they tramped back across the west forty for breakfast, Bill spotted a fox near the fencerow. Don quickly gave Bill the nod, for a fox can be a menace to the small lambs; the boy shot once and ran to pick up his prize. Seeing a small movement he drew back his foot to end the animal's suffering with a kick.

"No," warned Don. "A wounded animal can chew up your foot even with your heavy Red Wing boots. Shoot it again!"

"Dad, do you realize what these shells cost?" yelped Bill in outrage—even as he complied. It was too early in the season for the pelt to have any value, but that in no way diminished Bill's pleasure and pride. His voice was high-pitched with excitement as he called us to the dooryard and flung down his first "big game." Bruce mourned over the dainty fox, whose reddish fur was vivid in the morning sun. He came to cuddle against me on the steps where Anne and I had settled down to hear the stories over and over: how our steady new hunter had not flinched at the commotion of the pheasants' flight; how he never hesitated when the fox froze motionless in the sunshine for the briefest moment.

A wide stock gate opening into the dooryard had been left ajar as the hunters came in, and hearing a little rustle there, we looked up to see a ewe hesitantly entering. An intentness in her manner caught our attention and prevented our immediately chasing her out.

"Watch!" cautioned Don quietly, and we realized this was our Gem herself. She had smelled the fox and sensed danger to her young. Oblivious of us, she advanced stifflegged, head down, cautious, alert, belligerent. Suddenly she ran forward a few steps, stamping the ground noisily, and jumped aside. She retreated a bit, tested the air again and repeated the process. Each time she got a little closer. We observed the drama breathlessly. This was a sheep, symbol of passivity and helplessness! Another ewe, seeing the yard gate ajar, ventured near, then another and another—but each one, as she inhaled the dread scent, bolted. Then the flock, too, moved away uncaring. But Gem's attention was not diverted. In fact, she seemed not to notice. Like a statue of outraged motherhood, she stood with her head lowered, body tense, motionless as she stood within a foot of the poor lifeless rag of fur. Suddenly she lunged and butted clumsily. The threatening odor intensified, and, in a terrified frenzy, she butted repeatedly and struck with her front hooves.

Don now stepped up to calm her, but Bill, anxious about damage to the fox pelt, was already pulling her away. Together they talked to her, scratched her head, and quieted her. When they held the limp fox up by the tail, Gem was emboldened to sniff it thoroughly. Satisfied at last, she backed slowly off and trotted away to her triplets, waiting restlessly outside the buckthorn hedge.

Even as Bill proved his prowess as hunter and protector of his property, so the Great Earth Mother proved her courage as a hunter and defender of her young. For Don, however, his hunt for a buyer was still incomplete and his skill as a hunter unproved.

Three Bags Full and One Still Empty

Don put down the phone with an air of determination and turned to me. "This time, let's not let anything interfere with the children's taking part in shearing the sheep. I have a solid offer for the whole bunch, so they may not have another chance."

Don was proceeding resolutely on the assumption that the farm would be sold. Every time he went to town on business, he kept alert for new prospects and checked with his contacts. At the same time, he was feeling his way into setting up a real estate business. The children's participation in the shearing ritual seemed important for bringing their part of our farm experience to a close.

Papa used to say, "A sheep is the only animal I know that doesn't need to have an excuse to die—only an opportunity." Very few of our sheep died under our care. An average of one lamb per ewe is considered good. From one hundred ewes, we raised about 115 lambs the first year, and we kept up that average as the flock grew. While Don let the children help with dipping the sheep to kill ticks and with medicating them for disease control, it seemed that something—like visits or lessons—always interfered when the shearers came.

We made arrangements for the crew to spend most of a day shearing our flock, and the children waited impatiently until the day came. They were all eyes watching the chief shearer, Toby, and his crew set up their equipment in the barn and make electrical connections for their clippers. The men teased and laughed and enjoyed the children's proprietary interest. They slung a rubber belt about five inches wide from a heavy beam. It formed a loop at waist height. Not wanting to appear ignorant, Bill and Anne coaxed Bruce into asking its purpose.

"Oh, we hang the sheep up in that so they can't get away if they don't like their barber." Toby watched their reaction.

"But why isn't there one for each of you?" Bruce was observant.

"Oh, really, to tell the truth, it isn't for the sheep—it's a hammock for me." Toby was enjoying himself. "Do you want to try it?"

Cautious this time, Bruce didn't accept. All three watched every move as the men quickly fitted together a rectangular scaffold, about eight feet high, into which they hung a heavy canvas sack. They secured a ladder to the side of this arrangement under the intense scrutiny of the entrepreneurs. Toby looked at Anne, tall and quick in her movements.

"How'd you like to climb up there and drop the wool clips in for us?"

She nodded her willingness, but Bill had inherited his grandfather's need to tease.

"If you're resting in a hammock, there won't be much work for her."

"Now, maybe you're right. But I'll try hard to keep ahead of her. I'll just make you a bet that I can."

"I'd sure like to see how those clippers work."

"Okay. You'll have a chance when this is all finished. But right now I need a good, lively fellow to fold and tie the fleeces. Do you think you could handle that?"

As he spoke, the short, muscular crew chief lay forward into the hanging circle of heavy rubber, fitting it like a belt across his chest and under his arms. With his back relieved of strain, Toby proceeded to clip three sheep in the same amount of time it took his crew members to shear two. Bruce had been appointed "Opener of the Chute Gate," and he watched sympathetically as his pets stepped innocently out. Toby grabbed the first one, and with a firm, practiced twist flipped her onto her back where she lay immobile and silent. The electric clippers hummed around the face, cutting the wool off in little clumps. Then they moved over the body, leaving small ridged rows showing where the matted fleece had been peeled off—as if it were one continuous blanket.

Soon the children were too busy with their own jobs to watch. The dust, the rising heat, and the staccato bleating of the penned animals made the humans wish that they, too, could take off their coverings and run outside. Bill folded pelts and handed them up to Anne, who soon found it necessary to step down into the sack to tramp the ten-pound fleeces into a firm growing bundle. The men encouraged her, and Toby needled her constantly. "Have you caught up yet? What are you doing in there? I'm going to be done before you, you know!"

As the oldest, Anne was used to winning. She worked

so hard that she did not stop to think that she could hardly pack and tramp the last fleece until Toby had finished clipping it off and Bill had folded it. Bruce was triumphant as he "won," and Bill satisfied his mechanical bent by trying out the clippers. Anne's weariness vanished, although her dignity suffered, when two of the men called her a good sport and hoisted her to their shoulders. They were all pleased that the hot work had gone more quickly than they planned, and so they trooped to the kitchen where the afternoon snack of meat sandwiches, cinnamon rolls, coffee, and cherry nectar was transformed into a party. Toby orchestrated the playful joking and friendliness that kept the youthful owners in the center of the fun.

It was a happy day and one that the children long remembered. When Don sold the children's flock and wool, the proceeds paid off the residual debt of $2,200. There was enough remaining for Anne's freshman year at the University of Minnesota at Morris and for Bill there three years later. A tad was left to help Bruce at Hamline University in St. Paul when his turn came.

For Don it was another step in disposing of farm properties, and that made him happy. On the sale of the farm itself, however, he had no success. One potential sale, of course, had been irretrievably lost. The other he kept alive, but neither he nor the prospect found financial backing. The previous summer had been overly busy with a promising crop and not enough help, only to end with hail, which cut our yield in half. With his custom combining for neighboring farms, Don tried desperately to keep us on an even financial keel. However, some of the other farmers had been hit by hail too and were unable to pay for the work. The prospects were indeed bleak. The planting had been delayed by sleet and rain in that spring of 1958. Predictably restless, Don constantly rechecked the planter and tractors, returning to the house always chilled through. When his appetite became finicky, I attributed it to his frustration at not being able to plant on time. Soon, however, we realized he had the flu, and I could not persuade him to stay in bed. At every chance, he worked the least soggy fields or even parts of fields. Reports of flu came from all sides, and one Wednesday the buses brought the children home at noon. School had been closed for the remainder of the week. Bruce and I escaped the illness, but Bill was down for a few days, and Anne was content to find a quiet corner with a book. Don was determined to keep going. He doggedly cared for the stock and eventually succeeded in getting some planting done. As the weather warmed, seeds began to germinate, but the lines of green stitching on the black earth were broken and ragged. The unremitting struggle with fieldwork began to seem like an end in itself—chaotic, without purpose and with slim hope of reward, like an obbligato that overwhelms the melody.

This freak year of rain—the opposite of the drought that usually stalked us—was to continue with a vengeance throughout the summer. The 1958 crop was well on its dismal way before Don fully admitted to himself the reason for his lack of success in finding financial support for the sale of our farm. In spite of the fifteen-year upward trend of the Douglas fortunes, we were now in a poor bargaining position. By this time everyone knew we wanted to sell, and last year's hail, followed by the developing wet year, made it increasingly difficult. The bankers, instantly aware of their advantage, demanded more collateral for current loans on stock, machinery, and running expenses. New loans for farm purchase were set up in an way that almost assured they would be confiscated. In years past Mother Douglas, who had seen many farms foreclosed by greedy bankers, had a sharp edge to her voice whenever she spoke about small-town bankers. Don had many occasions to agree with her opinion in the coming months.

Grimly, he made up his mind to consider less favorable terms than he had hoped for. He returned to his local banker to discuss the possibility of extending the mortgage under the regulations of the current federal government program. He filled in the application and consulted with the banker and the lawyer who would supply additional information. The two men agreed to complete the application and call Don back within two weeks to sign it. Don hoped this arrangement would make it easier for our potential customer to assume the obligations of the farm.

The weather did not relent. We had experienced periods of raininess before, but a year this wet was unique in our experience. Grain and alfalfa grew stunted and thin. Soybeans turned yellow and then just rotted. What corn grew was sickly, runty with small stubby ears, if indeed it produced any ears at all.

When the closing date for making application approached, and Don received no summons from the bank, he took time to go to town, expecting to sign and send off the prepared application.

"What is it, Don? What can I do for you?" came the banker's greeting after Don waited to be called into his office.

"It's time to get that application signed and off to the federal office, and I'm here to do the job." Don's smile was forced, for something in the banker's attitude warned him of trouble.

"Oh, didn't the lawyer tell you? He was going to phone you. By the time we got all the information together, it was too late. That date we gave you was when the papers had to be acted on. The papers had to be there two weeks before, and we just didn't make it in time."

When my husband repeated this conversation to me, he also repeated a rumor—there are always rumors—that the lawyer's brother wanted the farm and hoped foreclosure would mean he could get it dirt cheap. Don was as close to despair as I had ever seen him. He even confessed at last that he, too, had sometimes hit bottom in making the adjustment back to farming. He remembered waking on his fortieth birthday, sitting up in bed and saying to himself, "Another year older, and I'm going out there and work like a dog till dark. Is this all there is to life?" Even the suggestion that another friend might have put self-interest above all else at such a crisis in our lives was unnerving. Did they figure that if we were moving away we were fair game?

I don't think either of us slept much that night. I, too, was upset that people we considered friends had apparently failed to support us when our luck was bad. But also

I felt concern about the effect it was having on Don. I needn't have worried. Don had unshakable ideals, but he was also a realist. He knew that not everyone had the same scale of values he did, not even people he cared about and trusted. He also knew that difference did not necessarily make them bad people—only different. He just needed to relate to them with a bit more caution. In a way, he seemed to be relieved to understand what was working against him. Determinedly, he widened the circle of neighboring towns he visited.

Full Circle

With the crop year drawing to an unprofitable close, our prospects looked decidedly dismal. We had committed to selling the farm and had disposed of stock and most of our hay and feed. If we borrowed to run the business in 1959, it would involve a higher interest rate, and the bank wanted even our car included in collateral. To take this step meant that we would have to forgo all our planning. To us, it seemed a big step backward, and each day without a sale brought us closer to that decision.

Late in 1958 an answer came to our dilemma. Jake Bruyness, a Hollander from Hardwick in southern Minnesota, was seeking a place for his father-in-law, Henry Berghorst, who wanted to come to Minnesota to start a dairy business. Jake had heard of our farm and came to visit it. He was most impressed with the two solid, recently painted hundred-foot barns. The land was also considerably cheaper per acre than the top-grade cropland he farmed. His banker proved to be ready to back the enterprise, and in no time they drew up a satisfactory arrangement for everyone. Although neither the sale nor the auction of machinery brought as much as we hoped, they provided security for our change and a new start.

Now we had to confront the move from our business, which was also the only home our children had ever known. The move—so long sought—proved to be wrenching and full of conflicting emotions.

I looked up at the sweep of sky where our great cottonwood tree once spread its branches. I missed its shelter and protection as I missed the love and care of our parents. Nevertheless, I felt ready for this passage into the vacant place in the front lines. Full adulthood comes to us through experiences common to all, but also through those peculiar events each of us has in our own time. I was happy, however, that our experiences had left us sure of ourselves and of each other—and eager for what lay ahead.

Because it was Anne's last year of high school and she wanted to graduate with her class, we decided to have a shakedown period. We rented a farm home a couple of miles to the north for the 1958–59 school year. Anne did well in her studies; she had a title part in the class play, we entertained the cast at a luncheon in our home, and her year finished with the senior prom.

Don tried a stint at farm real estate and had some success. One day I was surprised to hear him persuading an eager young man *not* to buy the farm for which he had loans arranged. The lad had not reckoned the additional money needed for stock, wages, machinery, and gasoline. The sale would have been a foreclosure in the making. Don could easily have concluded the deal instead of passing up the fee, which we could well have used. As it was, he had only a grateful young man for his trouble—and the knowledge that he would never be fully comfortable as a salesman. When an administrator of the Minnesota Department of Highways suggested that he apply for work as an appraiser, Don found a satisfying position protecting the interests of farmers when roads encroached on their land.

I renewed my social work contacts by working in the Morris welfare department for a few months. At Anne's graduation open house, over a hundred guests came to wish us well in our new life. It was a strange feeling that summer to watch Henry Berghorst with his wife and family of eleven children invade our house. We learned that they worked early and late, even missing school days when fieldwork was pressing. He filled our barns with a good Holstein herd and eventually, with income hard-won in the grueling dairy business, he would deepen the well and build a more spacious house.

For us, it was the right time for a change. Anne was a natural teacher and looked forward excitedly to the university. Bill had known for some time that his father was dissatisfied with the farm income and was restless to try new ventures. He had begun to feel the stirring of new ambitions as well—high school sports, jobs, and college.

The sheep shearing was still vivid in my mind as I pondered the great changes that we all now faced. I remembered how the sheep, after shedding their burden of wool, sprang joyfully away from their barbers. Like them, we all felt newly energized as the confining life of the farm slipped from us with the final sale of the property. In 1943 Don had been drawn by filial loyalty back to the life he knew as a boy, and I had strived mightily to throw off the clinging nostalgia of girlhood dreams. Now, seventeen years later, again poised on the threshold of a new life, I faced a new challenge. It was much like moving to my first job in New York City so long ago and then to the alien world of farming. Both experiences had given me a great rush of excitement, apprehension, and eagerness. Now, however, the new challenge was undergirded with a quiet self-confidence born of experience.

Each of us would face new and vastly different prospects. My circle from city to farm and back to city would be joined. It occurred to me that our children's impressionable years, like Don's, had been spent on the farm. I wondered whether they would sometime feel incomplete without a horse under them, or living near cattle and sheep grazing a rocky pasture with a sparkling stream running through it. Gradually we learned to face the move with enthusiasm only pleasantly tinged with reluctance. When we had sent the moving van loaded with our furniture and other possessions off to the Twin Cities and were ourselves loaded into the car, Don offered to take us to the farm. He paused at the entrance where the railroad tracks had trapped Donna's car on that anxious day so long ago. No one wanted to drive in to the farm, which was no longer ours. Memories were crowding. He pulled away, and for a long time we drove in silence.

By fall 1960 we were comfortably settled in a Minneapolis suburb, and I was caught up in the pursuits I sometimes yearned for in those busy years of farming. A new career in school social work had opened up for me in the Minneapolis elementary schools; Don continued his work with the highway department.

When Anne talked of the farm, her piano and her lovingly curried mare were at the top of the list. Bruce, then a fourth grader, warmly remembered pets, especially Spike, and his friends. Now Bruce planned for friends to visit him to swim and ride bikes in the city parks. Bill, perhaps more than the others, had absorbed the whole milieu. He had loved the freedom to tramp the countryside, with his dog running ahead. At age four he copied farm machinery in Tinker Toys; at ten he was helping his dad to repair it. By twelve, his mind had begun to invent improvements, and he dreamed of a car of his own to tinker with.

But what of Don and me? Don had always felt farming to be a proud calling. Working together and feeling needed had drawn the family close. Don's sturdy belief that a "good deal" must be good for both parties expanded to family and to the whole community. His parents who farmed, and mine who loved the lakes and woods, did not live to see the environmental awareness that grew out of this period—an awareness that brought such satisfaction to Don. He strove for limited use of pesticides and for soil and water conservation. He protested irrigation and even automatic dish washers and washing machines, and he urged those policies on his neighbors. He was president of the local Farm Bureau, but he laughingly called the Saturday night Whist Club his professional organization. In a way, it had become mine, too. There, with those people, I picked up many of the fine points of gardening, sewing, and farm cooking as we joked, gossiped, argued, and shared each other's troubles and dreams.

As with most mothers, I suspect, the strongest tug for me was still to those country friends with whom I shared my babies and agonized over our problems. With them I had built strong bonds that I now realize brought meaning to my life. But over the years the relationships between town and country have changed. No longer does the Whist Club stand for the country values of self-reliance and the Town Bridge Club signify complacent privilege. Farmers' reduced incomes force them and their wives to take part-time jobs in town, and business people realize anew their dependence on a healthy farm economy. More and more they share interests and work together on an equal footing in church and school and community.

In the old fairy tale the bluebird, symbol of happiness, is sought around the world and found at last in one's own backyard. My heart will always be where my family is, and it warms as I think of the peculiarly enriching experiences of those early years.

Like the mothhummingbird that darted among the blooms in the buckeye tree, my memory flits lightly over the hard work that focused our energies so relentlessly. It extracts only sweetness and fulfillment from our family's years on the farm.

Afterword

When Don and I retired from our jobs in the Twin Cities, we enjoyed traveling in our motor home, visiting friends and family. In 1979 Don had his first lung collapse after "forty years of good smoking." In the ten years that followed, we had many more trips, although Don's health was never again robust. He found time to help me get the business details of farming accurately onto paper for this book, and those years were good ones, too. In 1989, after a few days in the hospital—with no struggle, but with quiet dignity and acceptance—he left me.

The whole clan—children, grandchildren, brothers, their wives and children—all gathered in support and love with friends and members of our community church where we had so recently celebrated our fiftieth wedding anniversary. Losing him was like being torn in two. In the beginning, I felt frightened to be without his loving support. Even having only my own wishes to consider for the first time in my life felt uncomfortably foreign. Now, in my memory, Don and my old self take on fresh dimensions and deeper significance as my life expands in new directions.

Don and Marjorie at their fiftieth wedding anniversary, 1987

Anne became a teacher and lives in Massachusetts; her two daughters are near college graduation in child psychology and geology. Bill (who was sighted under his revved-up car one short hour before his wedding) is a credit manager for Toro Company and is still friend and helper to everyone. He and his wife and son live just around the corner from me; his daughter D'Anna (who changed her name from Anna, saying she wanted to keep the Douglas in her name) married two years ago and lives nearby, so I can enjoy my first great-grandchild, Tommie. Bruce and his family also live not far away. He is a customer service representative with Eastman Kodak. I call his daughters Snow White and Rose Red, because of their coloring; his youngest is a husky boy now eagerly exploring kindergarten.

In Bruce—idealistic, accommodating, and supportive—I sometimes see myself: the quiet, city girl who found a deep satisfaction in adapting to the vicissitudes and pleasures of country life with these children and their father.